W9-DJJ-695

Contemporary's

Writing and Reading the Essay

A Process Approach

Contemporary's

Writing and Reading the Essay

A Process Approach

Project Editor
Pat Fiene

CONTEMPORARY
BOOKS

CHICAGO

Some of the material that appears in this book also appears in
Contemporary's *Foundations Writing*. Copyright © 1993 by
Contemporary Books, Inc. (ISBN: 0-8092-3829-2)

Published by Contemporary Books, Inc.
Two Prudential Plaza, Chicago, Illinois 60601-6790
Manufactured in the United States of America
International Standard Book Number: 0-8092-4216-8

10   9   8   7   6   5   4   3

Published simultaneously in Canada by
Fitzhenry & Whiteside
195 Allstate Parkway
Markham, Ontario L3R 4T8
Canada

Editorial Director
Mark Boone

Writers
Pamela Bliss
Patricia Cronin
Virginia Lowe

Editorial
Christine M. Benton
Leah Mayes
Elena Anton
Lisa Black
Katherine Willhoite
Gerilee Hundt
Craig Bolt

Editorial Assistant
Maggie McCann

Editorial Production Manager
Norma Fioretti

Production Editor
Jean Farley Brown

Photography
C. C. Cain

Cover Design
Georgene Sainati

Art & Production
Sue Springston
Todd Petersen

Typography
Point West, Inc.
Carol Stream, Illinois

Cover photograph © C. C. Cain

CONTENTS

ACKNOWLEDGMENTS

"Running on the Beach," by Leah Kohlenberg, is reprinted by permission of the author.

"Mr. Ostrowski" is from *The Autobiography of Malcolm X* by Malcolm X as told to Alex Haley. Copyright © 1964 by Alex Haley and Malcolm X. Copyright © 1965 by Alex Haley and Betty Shabazz. Reprinted by permission of Random House, Inc.

"Chicken Parmesan McCurdy," by Alexander G. McCurdy, is reprinted by permission of the author.

"Pie Crust" is reprinted with the permission of Atheneum Publishers, an imprint of Macmillan Publishing Company, from *Iron Pots and Wooden Spoons*, by Jessica B. Harris. Copyright © 1989 by Jessica B. Harris.

"Improvements" is reprinted by permission of The Putnam Publishing Group for *The Osgood Files*, by Charles Osgood. Copyright © 1991 by Charles Osgood.

"Political Parties" is reprinted with the permission of Atheneum Publishers, an imprint of Macmillan Publishing Company, from *A Few Minutes with Andy Rooney*, by Andrew A. Rooney. Copyright © 1981 by Essay Productions, Inc.

"Why I Am for the Death Penalty," by Richard Myers, is reprinted by permission of the author.

"Why I Oppose the Death Penalty," by Steve Cline, is reprinted by permission of the author.

INTRODUCTION

Welcome to Contemporary's *Writing and Reading the Essay: A Process Approach*. This book will help you build your writing, reading, and thinking skills.

In Part I: Writing, you'll learn the process approach to writing and its four major stages:

▶ **Prewriting**—planning and organizing

▶ **Drafting**—writing according to plan

▶ **Revising**—evaluating and rewriting

▶ **Editing**—checking grammar, mechanics, and usage

You'll also learn how to read, analyze, and write short essays that describe, tell a story, explain, or persuade.

Part II: Grammar is a language-skills workbook. It explains the points of grammar, mechanics, and usage developing writers need to know. You can do a complete review of language skills by finishing all the exercises. Or, if you prefer, you can customize your review. Just do the Editing Exercise at the end of chapters 2–8. Each exercise covers a different part of speech or area of grammar. When you complete an exercise, check your answers against those in the Answer Key at the back of the book. If you miss an answer, the key will tell you what page to review. You also can use Part II as a handbook—a place where you can look up points of grammar when you write.

As you work through *Writing and Reading the Essay*, look for these special features:

▶ **With a Partner**—writing, reading, and thinking activities to do with a classmate, family member, or friend

▶ **In Your Journal**—ideas to think and write about on your own

▶ **Full-length essays** by Malcolm X, Andy Rooney, Leah Kohlenberg, and others

▶ A **Post-Test**, on pages 199–205, to help you see how well you've mastered the material in the book. The **Post-Test Answer Key** on pages 207–210 will help you evaluate your answers. By filling out the **Post-Test Evaluation Chart** on page 206, you'll see what skills to review.

We hope that you enjoy *Writing and Reading the Essay: A Process Approach*. We wish you the best of luck with your studies.

The Editors

PART I
WRITING

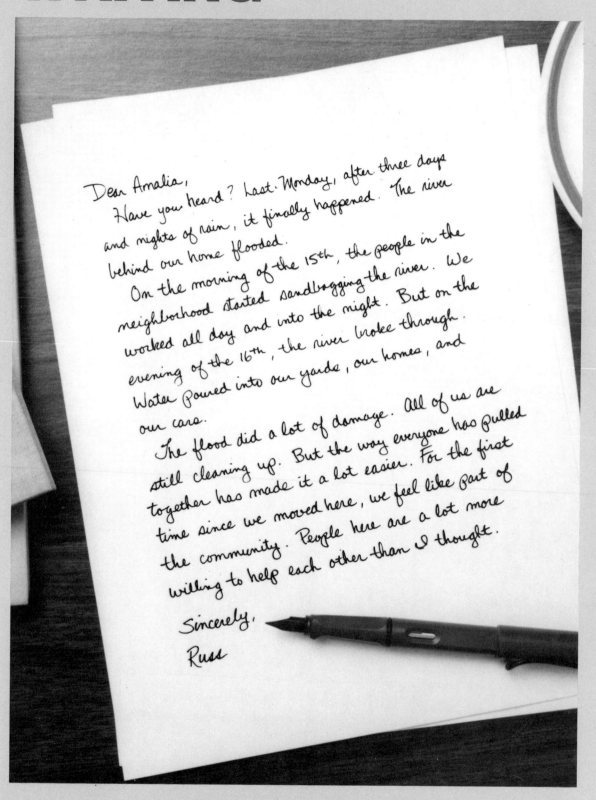

Dear Amalia,

Have you heard? Last Monday, after three days and nights of rain, it finally happened. The river behind our home flooded.

On the morning of the 15th, the people in the neighborhood started sandbagging the river. We worked all day and into the night. But on the evening of the 16th, the river broke through. Water poured into our yards, our homes, and our cars.

The flood did a lot of damage. All of us are still cleaning up. But the way everyone has pulled together has made it a lot easier. For the first time since we moved here, we feel like part of the community. People here are a lot more willing to help each other than I thought.

Sincerely,

Russ

CHAPTER 1 | THE ESSAY

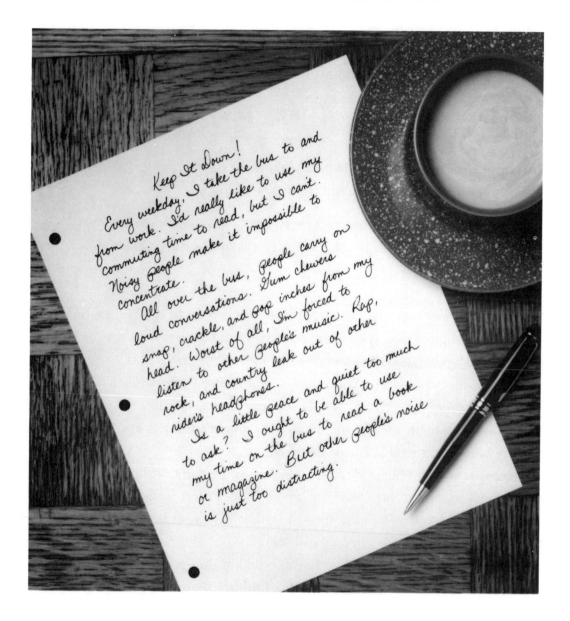

Keep It Down!

Every weekday, I take the bus to and from work. I'd really like to use my commuting time to read, but I can't. Noisy people make it impossible to concentrate.

All over the bus, people carry on loud conversations. Gum chewers snap, crackle, and pop inches from my head. Worst of all, I'm forced to listen to other people's music. Rap, rock, and country leak out of other rider's headphones.

Is a little peace and quiet too much to ask? I ought to be able to use my time on the bus to read a book or magazine. But other people's noise is just too distracting.

Read the short essay above, about a bus rider's complaint. Why does a writing book begin by having you read? Reading and writing go hand in hand. Good reading skills help you write well. And good writing skills help you become a better reader. This book will teach you how to read essays as you learn how to write them. In this chapter, you'll take a closer look at the essay form.

AFTER WORKING THROUGH THIS CHAPTER, YOU SHOULD BE ABLE TO

▶ NAME THE THREE PARTS OF AN ESSAY
▶ DESCRIBE THE PURPOSE OF EACH PART
▶ FIND THE MAIN IDEA OF AN ESSAY

■ The Parts of an Essay

A good essay has a clear beginning, middle, and end. Writers call these parts the introduction, the body, and the conclusion. All three parts of an essay have one thing in common. All three are about the same main idea.

The Introduction

The **introduction** of an essay tells you what the essay is about. Reread the first paragraph of the essay at the beginning of this chapter.

> Every weekday, I take the bus to and from work. I'd really like to use my commuting time to read, but I can't. Noisy people make it impossible to concentrate.

Can you see how this first paragraph introduces you to the rest of the essay? The first sentence gives you the **topic**, or subject of the essay. In this case, the topic is *bus rides*. The second sentence tells you a little more about the topic. It lets you know that the writer has a complaint about riding on the bus. Then, in the last sentence, the writer says, "Noisy people make it impossible to concentrate." This sentence states the main idea of the essay. The **main idea** lets you know more specifically what the writer will say about the topic.

As you can see, the main idea narrows down the topic. It limits the subject to a point or points that the writer wants to make. The writer of the bus essay has narrowed the topic to one main point—the other riders on the bus make too much noise.

Early on, the writer gave you a clue as to what the main idea would be. Notice that the essay is titled "Keep It Down!" This title briefly tells you what point the writer will make. But also notice that a title doesn't take the place of a main idea. The writer must also put the main idea in a sentence or two in the introduction.

A GOOD INTRODUCTORY PARAGRAPH DOES TWO IMPORTANT THINGS:

▶ Introduces the topic
▶ States the main idea

Exercise 1

PART A

Read the essay. Then underline the main idea in the introduction.

Who's Hiring?

Getting a job begins with finding a job opening. You can find job openings in a number of ways.

Check the want ads in your local newspaper. Don't be afraid to ask friends and relatives if they know of any jobs. Call companies that you know you'd like to work for. And register with government and private job agencies.

These suggestions will help you find out who's hiring. And that's the first step toward finding a job.

PART B

Read this middle and end of an essay. Then circle the letter of the paragraph that would make a good introduction.

ABCs of Interviewing

Above all, be on time. You don't have to wear expensive clothes. But do dress neatly. Act confident. Look the interviewer in the eye, and answer questions completely and honestly. Show that you know you can do the job.

A successful interview can bring you the job you want. Follow the guidelines above, and you'll find yourself in that job!

(a) While interviewing can be nerve-wracking, it can also give you a chance to make a good first impression. Make the most of your chance. Make sure you know what to do on job interviews.

(b) Job interviews can make you very nervous. Answering questions isn't easy. Sometimes you even have to go back for a second interview. Try to stay calm.

Check your answers on page 211.

The Body

The **body** of an essay tells more about the main idea. Reread the middle paragraph of the bus essay. As you read, think about the main idea of the essay: Other riders make too much noise.

> All over the bus, people carry on loud conversations. Gum chewers snap, crackle, and pop inches from my head. Worst of all, I'm forced to listen to other people's music. Rap, rock, and country leak out of other riders' headphones.

Can you see how the body explains the main idea? Each sentence gives examples of noisy riders. The ideas in the body of an essay are called **supporting details**. That is because they help support, or explain, the main idea. The diagram shows how a main idea and supporting details relate to each other.

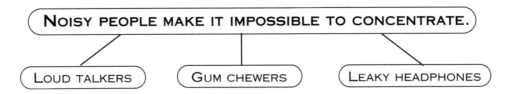

Each detail in the body tells a little more about the main idea. Each detail helps the reader understand what the writer means.

THE BODY OF AN ESSAY DOES ONE IMPORTANT THING:
▶ Supports the main idea

WITH A PARTNER

Get together with another person. Tell the person to imagine that he or she is going to write an essay. Ask the person one of the main idea questions below. Explain that each answer could be a detail in the body of an essay.

▶ What are five things you'd do if you won a million dollars?
▶ What are five things you'd hate to live without?
▶ What are five things you'd like to be remembered for?

When your partner is finished, have the person ask you one of the questions.

Exercise 2

PART A

Read the essay. (The main idea is underlined.) Then list the three main supporting details.

My Dream Home

My dream home would be a nice bungalow on the north side. There are many things that I'd like this home to have. <u>But three stand out above the rest.</u>

First, I want the home to have two bedrooms. Then my son, Louis, could have his own room and wouldn't have to sleep on the couch. I also want the house to have a big basement. That way, my husband, Big Lou, would have space to set up a workshop. Finally, I'd like the living room to have a fireplace. I've always loved how fireplaces make rooms feel cozy.

I may never get such a home for my family. But I can dream, can't I?

What are three things that the woman would like her house to have? List these supporting details.

(a) _____

(b) _____

(c) _____

PART B

Read this introduction to an essay. (The main idea is underlined.) Then circle the letter of the body that develops the main idea.

Everybody has a different idea about what the ideal home should be. My dream home would be a great apartment in a high-rise downtown. <u>I'd like to live there for a lot of reasons.</u>

(a) I'm a single guy from a small town. I moved to this city because I got a job here. I work for a large downtown insurance company. There are a lot of high-rise apartment buildings downtown.

(b) If I lived in a downtown high-rise, I'd be where all the action is. I would also have a great view of the lake, which is only a few blocks from the downtown. And I wouldn't have to commute to work. I'd live near enough to walk.

Check your answers on page 211.

The Conclusion

The **conclusion** sums up the main idea of the essay. Reread the last paragraph of the bus essay. Can you see how this final paragraph restates the writer's message?

> Is a little peace and quiet too much to ask? I ought to be able to use my time on the bus to read a book or magazine. But other people's noise is just too distracting.

The first two sentences emphasize the point that the writer wants to make. The last sentence restates the main idea: "Noisy people make it impossible to concentrate."

Notice that the conclusion doesn't bring up new ideas. For example, it doesn't tell about any other bus problems, like late buses or high fares. Instead, the conclusion "wraps up" the main idea that has already been explained.

A CONCLUDING PARAGRAPH DOES ONE IMPORTANT THING:
▶ Sums up the main idea of the essay

WITH A PARTNER

Think of a famous person whom you admire. "Sum up" the person by listing five or six important details that describe the person. Then read your list to someone else. Ask the person to guess whom you're describing. The better your summary, the more likely the person will be able to guess right.

Exercise 3

PART A

Read the essay. (The main idea has been underlined.) Then underline the sentence in the conclusion that restates the main idea.

The Day My World Fell Apart

Three years ago, my wife asked me for a divorce. <u>The day she confronted me was the worst of my life</u>.

At first, I couldn't believe it. I felt sick to my stomach. Then, I demanded to know why. She told me, and I tried to understand. But I still felt sick.

My world seemed to turn upside down the day LaTise asked for a divorce. Three years later, I'm still trying to cope with the loss.

PART B

Read this introduction and body of an essay. (The main idea has been underlined.) Then circle the letter of the conclusion that restates the main idea.

A Necessary Evil

The hardest thing I ever did was tell my husband I wanted a divorce. I hated to do it. <u>But the divorce was really necessary</u>.

We hadn't truly loved each other for a long time. We argued far too often. He got on my nerves, and I got on his. We were just living together. We weren't really a husband and wife working and loving together.

(a) Divorce is never easy. My divorce was especially tough. My brother and his wife also got divorced last year. They should have tried harder to work out their problems.

(b) A divorce was really best for both of us. I'm now a happy single woman instead of a miserable Mrs. My ex-husband is happier being unmarried too.

Check your answers on page 211.

■ The Longer Essay

So far, you've been analyzing very short essays. The essay below follows the pattern you've been studying. It was written by a worker who wanted to convince his company to make a change. As you read the essay, think about the three main parts.

Sample Three-Paragraph Essay

Introduction

It's About Time

The Waller Company should use flextime to schedule working hours. With flextime, workers would have some say over what time their workday starts and ends. Flextime would benefit both the company and the workers.

> MAIN IDEA

Body

For example, flextime would help some workers who have children. It also would be good for workers who are "early birds." And the company would benefit because the traffic problem in the parking lot would be solved.

> SUPPORTING DETAILS

Conclusion

Clearly, the Waller Company should switch to flextime. This method of scheduling benefits us all.

> RESTATEMENT OF MAIN IDEA

In many ways, the essay is good. It has an introductory paragraph with a clear main idea. The main idea is restated in the conclusion. And the body is made up of details that support the main idea.

But notice that the supporting details aren't fully explained. For example, the writer says that flextime would help some workers who have children. But it's not yet clear why it would help. You might be able to guess why, but you shouldn't have to. The writer should make the detail clear for you. In other words, he should further **develop** the body with more specific details.

Sample Longer Essay

Here is a longer, more fully developed version of the three-paragraph essay you just read. The longer essay has the same introduction and conclusion as the other essay. But the body has been expanded. Now, each supporting detail is explained in its own paragraph. Each supporting detail has specific details of its own.

Introduction

It's About Time

The Waller Company should use flextime to schedule working hours. With flextime, workers would have some say over what time their workday starts and ends. <u>Flextime would benefit both the company and the workers</u>.

> MAIN IDEA

Body

<u>For example, flextime would help some workers who have children.</u> Many working parents have trouble getting their children to daycare early in the morning. This is especially true for parents who travel by bus or train. Workers who have this problem could choose to start later than 8:00 A.M. They could start at 9:30 A.M. and work until 5:30 P.M.

> SUPPORTING DETAIL

<u>Flextime also would be good for workers who are "early birds."</u> These early risers are more productive in the morning. Therefore, they'd be better off starting quite early, such as 6:30 A.M., and ending early, such as 2:30 P.M.

> SUPPORTING DETAIL

The company would also benefit from flextime. That's because the <u>traffic problem in the parking lot would be solved.</u> Right now, everyone is trying to enter or leave the parking lot at the same time. With flextime, that would no longer be the case.

> SUPPORTING DETAIL

Conclusion

Clearly, the Waller Company should switch to flextime. <u>This method of scheduling benefits us all.</u>

> RESTATEMENT OF MAIN IDEA

The essay is now much easier to understand. It's also more convincing. By adding more details, the writer has built a stronger case for flextime.

Sometimes, a main idea can be fully explained in just three paragraphs. But in many cases, writers need more than three paragraphs to make their point.

Exercise 4

PART A

Read the essay. Underline the main idea sentence in the introduction. Underline the main supporting detail sentence in each paragraph in the body. Then underline the sentence that restates the main idea in the conclusion.

The Good Boss

Over the years, I've worked with many different bosses. As a result of working with them, I've learned what it takes to be a good boss.

First of all, a good boss is fair. He or she treats everyone equally. No employee is given better treatment than the others or allowed to goof off.

A good boss also doesn't overload employees with work. Sometimes, people may have to work overtime. Or they may have to work extra hard to meet a deadline. But a good boss makes sure the amount of work is reasonable.

Finally, a good boss knows how to motivate people. He or she is quick to compliment people on good work. At the same time, a good boss is quick to criticize sloppy work. If someone's work isn't done right, a good boss will talk to that person in private. He or she will try to get the best out of everyone.

In short, a good boss is fair, reasonable, and a good motivator. It's not easy to have all of these qualities. If your boss has them, you're a lucky employee.

PART B

Complete the essay by following the directions in each part.

Introduction

Most people would change some things about themselves if they only could. Some people wish they were more patient. Others wish that they were taller or thinner. Here are the three things I'd most like to change about myself.

Write your own supporting details in the blanks.

First,_____ ._____

Second,_____ ._____

Third,_____ ._____

First Paragraph of Body

Write a paragraph explaining your first supporting detail.

_____

_____

_____

_____

Second Paragraph of Body

Write a paragraph explaining your second supporting detail.

_____

_____

_____

_____

Third Paragraph of Body

Write a paragraph explaining your third supporting detail.

_____

_____

_____

_____

Conclusion

Write a paragraph that sums up the content of the body and restates the main idea.

_____

_____

_____

_____

Check your answers on page 211.

IN YOUR JOURNAL

From time to time, this book asks you to write in a journal. A **journal** is a notebook of private writing. In it, you jot down your thoughts about subjects of interest to you. Your journal is a place where you can practice writing. Your journal can also serve as a book of writing ideas. When you have an assignment but can't think of anything to say, thumb through your journal. See what topics you've already written about. Here are guidelines for creating a journal of your own.

▶ **If you can, write in a three-ring or spiral-bound notebook.**

You're less likely to lose pages if you write in a notebook.

▶ **Make journal writing a habit.**

Write in your journal every day (or as often as you can). The more you write, the more comfortable you'll become about writing.

▶ **Write about subjects that matter to you.**

Describe your wildest hopes and your deepest fears. Write down what you'd like to say to your boss, your teacher, or your family. Any subject that's on your mind is a good choice for journal writing.

▶ **Don't worry about length.**

Make each entry as long or as short as you like. Begin writing when you have an idea. Stop when you've run out of things to say.

▶ **Don't worry about making mistakes.**

Your journal is for your eyes only (unless you choose to show it to someone else). As a result, you don't need to worry about errors when you write in it. In addition, feel free to experiment with different forms. Try writing short stories, letters, or poems. Don't be afraid to try out new ideas.

▶ **Use your journal as a storehouse of ideas.**

Staple in items that you might like to write about someday. Store newspaper stories, pictures, cartoons, quotations, words to songs, or other items of interest.

▶ **Begin keeping a journal today.**

Here is a topic to get you started. Write about it—or think up a topic of your own. *If you could trade places with anybody for a day, who would it be? Why?*

CHAPTER 2 | THE WRITING PROCESS

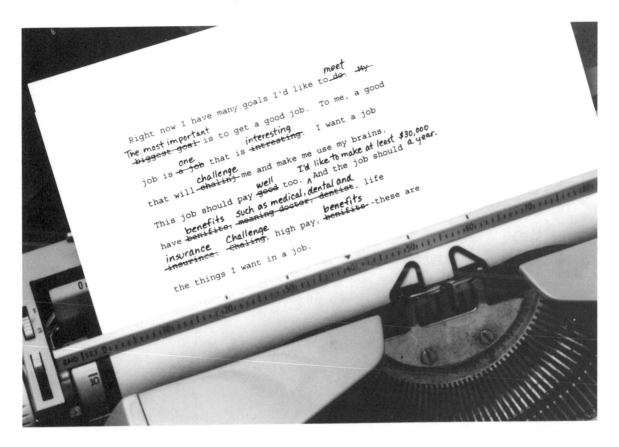

Writing is a process. Writers don't complete a good essay in one step. Instead, they go through different stages to get their ideas on paper clearly and logically. Like the student who wrote the paragraph above, writers may make many changes along the way. This chapter is a step-by-step guide to planning, writing, and rewriting essays.

As you work through this chapter, you will practice each of the four major stages in the process of writing:

▶ PREWRITING

▶ DRAFTING

▶ REVISING

▶ EDITING

Prewriting

PREWRITING	DRAFTING	REVISING	EDITING	FINAL DRAFT

Planning is the first stage in the writing process. This stage is called **prewriting** because you do it *before* you actually write. To plan an essay, you take these steps:

▶ Select a topic and purpose

▶ Develop the topic

▶ Organize your ideas

Prewriting is a flexible process. Though you need to do all of the steps above, the order you do them in may vary. Try following the order given in this chapter. If the order doesn't work well for you, change it to suit your needs.

Selecting a Topic and Purpose

Begin planning an essay by choosing a subject to write about. Select your topic carefully. A well-chosen topic can make you *want* to write. A poorly chosen topic can make writing seem hard—and boring.

For the assignments in this book, choose topics that you already know a lot about. You'll find it easier to write when you have plenty to say. Also, make sure that your topics interest you. The more interesting the topic, the more fun it is to write about.

In addition to a topic, you need a purpose, or reason for writing. Do you want to explain something? Describe someone or something? Tell the story of an experience you've had? Persuade someone to do something or believe something? Explaining, describing, telling a story, and persuading are the four main purposes you'll work with in this book. When you decide on a purpose, let your background, experiences, and interests be your guide.

For example, suppose that you like baseball. If you're good at playing the sport, you might share your know-how. You might explain how to pitch or bunt.

What if you don't play but love to watch the game? You might describe an afternoon at the ballpark. Make your readers know what it feels like to sit in the stands.

Have you ever watched a game that was decided in the last few seconds of play? You might tell the story of the exciting win.

Do you think baseball is a better sport than football? You might try to convince football fans to share your point of view.

As you can see, purpose affects content. When you know *why* you're writing, you'll also have a clearer picture of what you need to say.

Exercise 1

PART A

Put a check mark next to topics that you'd like to write about.

☐ music	☐ cooking	☐ politics	☐ dating	☐ nature
☐ TV	☐ cars	☐ religion	☐ work	☐ education
☐ movies	☐ sports	☐ family	☐ travel	☐ money
☐ dancing	☐ fashion	☐ children	☐ hobbies	☐ friendship

PART B

Select *one* of the topics that you checked in Part A. Decide on a purpose (to explain, to describe, to tell a story, or to persuade). On another piece of paper, explain what you plan to say. Follow the example below.

Topic: _Cars_

Purpose: _To describe_

What I plan to say: _I'm going to write about what it's like to drive my Miata. I'm going to describe the car inside and out. I'm going to write about how fast the car can go, how smooth the ride is, and how it feels to drive with the top down._

Answers will vary.

IN YOUR JOURNAL

Where can you find good ideas to write about? Many times, you can find them in simple, everyday events. When something captures your interest, jot down your ideas in your journal. Later, when you need a topic, look over your notes. You may want to expand on the topic in an essay.

Start creating a pool of ideas now. Choose *one* of the following "everyday" topics. Then write about it in your journal.

▶ An interesting item you heard on a TV or radio show

▶ A funny (or sad) item you read in the newspaper

▶ Something beautiful that you saw on a walk or drive

▶ An interesting talk you had with a friend

▶ A dream or nightmare

Developing the Topic

You've decided on a topic and a purpose for writing. What should you do next? Think of supporting details to develop the topic. Sometimes, ideas come quickly and easily. Other times, you may need help developing your thoughts. When you have trouble thinking of details to explain your topic, try brainstorming, questioning, or freewriting.

Brainstorming

When you **brainstorm**, you quickly list all your ideas about a subject. Your goal is to come up with as many ideas as you can. You don't take time to judge whether each detail is good or bad. You don't worry about spelling or grammar. You just set a time limit and write down every idea that comes to mind.

Here's a list a student brainstormed about the topic of home security. Her purpose was to explain how people can burglarproof their homes before leaving for vacation.

Topic and Purpose: <u>Explain how to make your home secure</u>

<u>1. Lock all doors and windows.</u>

<u>2. Stop mail delivery or have trusted neighbor pick it up.</u>

<u>3. Put lights on timer so they go on and off at usual times.</u>

<u>4. Ask trusted friend or neighbor to keep an eye on the house.</u>

<u>5. If you have an answering machine, have friend take phone messages and rewind tape if you can't do so.</u>

Exercise 2

Brainstorm about the topic and purpose you chose on page 17.

Topic and Purpose: _____

_____

_____

_____

_____

_____

Answers will vary.

Questioning

Another good way to develop supporting details is **questioning**. When reporters write stories, they ask questions that begin with these words: *Who? What? Where? When? Why? How?* These questions are known as the five Ws and an H. The answers to these questions are details that explain news stories. You can use the five Ws and an H to list details you need to explain a topic.

Here's how a student answered the five Ws and an H for his topic and purpose.

Topic and Purpose: _To describe my idea of the ideal day_

Who? _My girlfriend and I_

What? _Go to the Super Bowl_

Where? _The stadium where it's being held_

When? _Super Bowl Sunday_

Why? _To see the game_

How? _Fly to where it's being held_

Questioning also is good for adding to a brainstorming list. If you run out of ideas while brainstorming, further develop your list by asking the five Ws and an H.

Exercise 3

....

How would you spend your ideal day? Answer the five Ws and an H.

Who? _____

What? _____

Where? _____

When? _____

Why? _____

How? _____

Answers will vary.

Freewriting

You've now tried two ways to develop a topic—brainstorming and questioning. A third way to think of ideas is **freewriting**.

To freewrite, set a short time limit. Then write *nonstop* about your topic. Do not lift your pen from the page. If you run out of things to say, write the same word over and over until a thought comes to mind. It's OK if your thoughts wander from topic to topic. Just keep your pen moving and your ideas flowing.

Here's an example of freewriting about a specific topic and purpose.

Topic and Purpose: *To describe my idea of the ideal day*

Take it nice and slow. Sleep really late. Maybe have breakfast in bed. Have a servant bring me breakfast. Eat, eat, eat, eat, maybe music. Put on my favorite CDs and blast away the neighbors. Better yet, go see my favorite groups in person. Fly to New York. Have a limo pick me up and drive me to Manhattan.

Freewriting showed the student that she had plenty to say about her topic. If she had had little to say, she might have changed to a different topic or purpose.

Freewriting also is a good way to find a topic and purpose. If you can't think of a subject, try freewriting about an interesting picture in a magazine. Or freewrite about a person, place, or problem that's on your mind. Then look over what you wrote to see what topics you can find.

The following freewriting was done by a student who needed a topic and purpose for writing. When she started, she couldn't think of anything to say. Notice that she just repeated her name until a thought came to mind. One thought led to another, and she ended up with several topics that she might write about:

▶ how she used to feel about her name and how she feels now
▶ how much children need to feel that they belong
▶ how her grandmother's talents were passed on to her

Naidaj Naidaj Naidaj Naidaj Naidaj I used to hate my name. Nobody spelled it right and nobody seemed to know how to spell it. When I was little, the other kids made fun of it. It's funny how kids will pick on anything that's different. Kids want to be just like each other and to belong. Now I love my name. I'm named after my grandmother. Like her, I'm good at music.

Exercise 4

On another piece of paper, freewrite for five minutes about this picture. If you have trouble getting started, combine questioning with freewriting. Use your imagination to write answers to these questions: Who? What? Where? When? Why? How?

Answers will vary.

WITH A PARTNER

Imagine that you're a reporter, and make a list of interview questions you'd like to ask a classmate or friend. Begin each question with one of the five Ws and an H. Use the questions to interview your partner. Then write the interview in a question-and-answer format.

Organizing Your Ideas

Brainstorming, questioning, and freewriting will help you think of details to develop a topic. The next—and final—stage in prewriting is to **organize** your ideas. During this stage, you begin to shape your ideas into essay form. First, you write your main idea sentence. Then, you plan the body of your essay by grouping your ideas. When you're finished, your writing plan is complete.

Writing a Main Idea Sentence

An essay usually contains a main idea sentence. This sentence lets readers know what an essay is about.

Writing a main idea sentence will help you collect your thoughts. It also will give you a headstart on your introduction and conclusion. Recall that most introductions are built around a main idea sentence. And most conclusions contain a restatement of the main idea.

Sometimes, your main idea will be clear to you as soon as you think of a topic and purpose. Other times, it may take longer to decide what point or points you want to make. When you have trouble deciding on a main idea, think about your topic and purpose. Look over your supporting details. Then ask yourself, What are most of the details about? The answer to this question is the main idea.

Ask the question to find the main idea of this brainstormed list. Then put the main idea in sentence form.

Topic and purpose: To explain how to lose weight

▶ Losing weight helps your heart.
▶ Don't eat a lot of sugar.
▶ Set a weekly weight-loss goal.
▶ Talk yourself out of overeating.

▶ Stay away from fatty foods.
▶ Drink plenty of water.
▶ Picture yourself as thin.
▶ It's hard but worth it.

What are most of the details about? Most of them are ways to lose weight. A good main idea sentence might say this: Here are some ways to lose those extra pounds.

Exercise 5

PART A

Write a main idea sentence for each list of details.

1. Topic and Purpose: To explain how to quit smoking
- ▶ Stay away from smokers.
- ▶ Chew gum.
- ▶ Eat in no-smoking areas.
- ▶ Suck on sugarless candy.
- ▶ Go for walks.
- ▶ Do breathing exercises.

Main idea sentence: _____

_____

2. Topic and Purpose: To persuade people to walk rather than drive
- ▶ It's relaxing.
- ▶ It doesn't cause pollution.
- ▶ It saves money on gasoline.
- ▶ It's good exercise.

Main idea sentence: _____

_____

3. Topic and Purpose: To tell the story of my graduation day
- ▶ I woke up with a sore throat and fever.
- ▶ We had tornado warnings, and it poured all day.
- ▶ The dry cleaners accidentally gave my suit to someone else.
- ▶ The car got a flat tire, so I was late for the ceremony.
- ▶ I tripped and fell as I started to walk across the stage.

Main idea sentence: _____

_____

PART B

Look over the brainstorming, questioning, and freewriting that you did in this chapter. Choose one of the three, and write a main idea sentence for it.

Main idea sentence: _____

_____

Check your answers on page 211.

Grouping Ideas

Writing a main idea sentence will help you plan the introduction and conclusion of your essay. **Grouping ideas** will help you plan the body. When you group your ideas, you picture how the body will look. You decide whether it should be one, two, three, or more paragraphs.

To group ideas into paragraphs, look carefully at the supporting details you've developed. Sometimes, all your details will be closely related to each other. They form one group, or paragraph. But other times, your details may be divided into two or more groups. Then, you'll need more than one paragraph for the body.

One way to group ideas is to draw a line around the details that go together.

Main idea sentence: Here are some ways to lose those extra pounds.

▶ Eat complex carbohydrates — eating
▶ ~~Losing weight helps your heart.~~
▶ Stay away from fatty food.
▶ Don't eat a lot of sugar.
▶ Drink plenty of water.
▶ Set a weekly weight-loss goal.
▶ Picture yourself as thin.
▶ Talk yourself out of overeating.
▶ ~~It's hard but worth it.~~
mental

Notice that the writer put the details into two groups, or paragraphs. She labeled one group "eating," because all the details are about good eating habits. She labeled the other group "mental," because all the details are about how to prepare mentally to lose weight. Some of the details didn't fit into any group, so the writer crossed them out. Also, as she was grouping ideas, the writer thought of another supporting detail—eat foods high in complex carbohydrates. So she added it to the list.

Some writers prefer to draw clusters to picture how main ideas and details relate to each other. Here's a cluster of the same list of details. In the center is the main idea. Attached to the main idea are the two clusters, or groups of details.

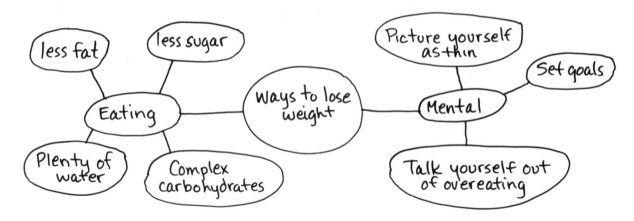

Exercise 6

PART A

Finish putting the ideas in the lists into the correct groups or clusters.

1. Main idea sentence: I have mixed feelings about getting my own apartment.

▶ ~~could come and go as I please~~
▶ ~~will cost a lot~~
▶ would feel good to be on my own
▶ would have my own bathroom and bedroom
▶ might be kind of lonely
▶ could play my music whenever I want
▶ hate to cook and clean

Group A: Good Points
(a) could come and go as I please

(b)

(c)

(d)

Group B: Bad Points
(a) will cost a lot

(b)

(c)

2. Main idea sentence: I get many benefits from exercising.

▶ ~~feel calmer—helps me cope with stress~~
▶ ~~keeps my weight under control~~
▶ feel more confident because I look better
▶ proud of sticking to my exercise plan
▶ have fewer aches and pains
▶ have more energy

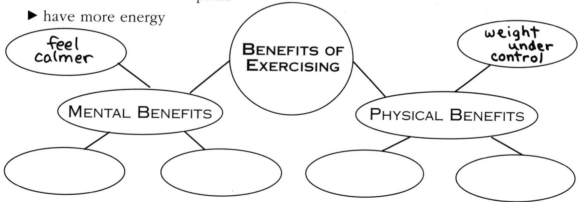

PART B

On another piece of paper, group the details that go with the main idea sentence you wrote on page 23. Circle the details that go together, or draw a cluster or clusters.

Check your answers on page 211.

 Drafting

PREWRITING	DRAFTING	REVISING	EDITING	FINAL DRAFT

You've practiced all the steps in prewriting. Your writing plan is now complete. You're ready to begin the second stage of the writing process—**drafting,** or writing.

Your first version of an essay is called the **first draft**. The purpose of this draft is to get your ideas on paper in essay form. It's OK if the first draft is somewhat rough and unpolished. It's also OK if it has spelling errors or other kinds of mistakes. You'll have chances to improve and correct the draft when you revise and edit.

Drafting from a Plan

As you write your first draft, follow the plan you created during freewriting. The example below shows, step by step, how to write from a plan. (You may notice a few spelling errors and other mistakes in the sample first draft. You'll have a chance to correct them later.)

Step 1: Build an introduction around the main idea sentence.

Often, the introduction of an essay begins with an interesting sentence or two. These sentences help get readers' attention and lead them to the main idea. The introduction then ends with the main idea sentence.

Writing Plan

Main Idea Sentence

Here are some ways to lose those extra pounds.

Sample First Draft

Introduction

Are you tired of being overwieght? Would you like to look and feel better? Here are some ways to lose those extra pounds.

Step 2: Write the body using the details in your groups or clusters.

Turn each group or cluster into a paragraph.

Cluster 1

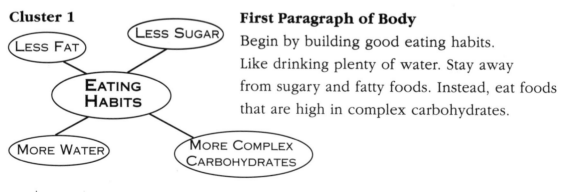

First Paragraph of Body

Begin by building good eating habits. Like drinking plenty of water. Stay away from sugary and fatty foods. Instead, eat foods that are high in complex carbohydrates.

Cluster 2

TALK YOURSELF OUT OF OVEREATING

MENTAL HABITS

SET GOALS

PICTURE YOURSELF THIN

Second Paragraph of Body

Its also important to prepare yourself mentally. Each week, set a realisitic weight-loss goal. That way, you have something specific to aim for. When your tempted to overeat, talk yourself out of it. Picture the thin person inside yourself just waiting to get out.

Step 3: Build a conclusion around a restatement of the main idea.

Write an interesting sentence or two that leads to a restatement of the main idea. Then end with the restatement.

Main Idea Sentence

Here are some good ways to lose those extra pounds.

Conclusion

Losing weight isn't easy. But you can do it if you really want to and know how. Follow the methods in this essay, and you, too, will lose weight.

Exercise 7

On another piece of paper, write a first draft of the essay you planned in Exercise 6, Part B, page 25.

Answers will vary.

Revising

| PREWRITING | DRAFTING | REVISING | EDITING | FINAL DRAFT |

You've written a draft of an essay, but it's a first draft. To begin making it a final draft, you work through the third stage of the writing process: revising.

When you **revise**, you take a second look at what you've written. You evaluate your essay to see how it might be improved. Then you rewrite any problem areas.

Many writers also like to have someone else read their first drafts. Getting another person's opinion can be very helpful. No matter how careful you are, it's easy to overlook your own weaknesses. Many writers also find it helpful to use a checklist when they revise. That way, they can easily keep track of all they want to look for.

As a part of revising, the writer of the weight-loss essay gave her draft to a classmate to read. He used the following Revision Checklist to evaluate her work.

☞ Revision Checklist

Yes No

☑ ☐ **1.** Does the essay have an introductory paragraph or paragraphs?

☑ ☐ **2.** Is the main idea clearly stated in the introduction?

☑ ☐ **3.** Does the body contain at least one paragraph?

☐ ☑ **4.** Does the body contain enough details to develop the main idea?

☑ ☐ **5.** Do all the details in the body support the main idea?

☑ ☐ **6.** Are the details in the body logically organized?

☑ ☐ **7.** Is there a paragraph or paragraphs of conclusion?

☑ ☐ **8.** Does the conclusion help sum up the main idea?

☐ ☑ **9.** Are all the sentences and ideas clear?

Notice that the evaluator felt the body needed further development. He suggested that the writer add something about exercise, because it's an important part of weight loss. In addition, the evaluator pointed out some ideas that weren't clear. For example, the writer said that dieters should drink "plenty" of water. But she didn't say why—or how much. The writer's revisions are on the next page.

Take It Off!

Are you tired of being overwieght? Would you like to look and feel better? Here
are some ways to lose those extra pounds.

Begin by building good eating habits. Like drinking ~~plenty of water.~~ Stay away
at least five glasses of water a day.
(Water will help cut your appetite.)
from sugary and fatty foods. Instead, eat foods that are high in complex
Also,

carbohydrates. *, such as potatoes or pasta.

Its also important to prepare yourself mentally. Each week, set a realisitic
weight-loss goal. *For example, say you'll try to lose one pound.* That way, you have something specific to aim for. When your

tempted to overeat, talk yourself out of it. Picture the thin person inside yourself

just waiting to get out. *You also should try to exercise each day. Walk instead of driving. Climb the stairs instead of using the elevator.*

Losing weight isn't easy. But you can do it if you really want to and know how.

Follow the methods in this essay, and you, too, will lose weight.

Exercise 8

PART A

Answer the questions on the Revision Checklist to evaluate this essay.

Just One Job?

After I graduated from high school, I went right to work. I am a secretary for
three lawyers.

I do the work of many people. When I enter letters and legal papers on the
computer, I am a word processor. When I correct the lawyers' spelling and
grammar mistakes, I do the work of an English teacher. I am a travel agent
when I make plane and hotel reservations for my bosses. And I am a mental
health worker when I listen to their problems and offer advice.

PART B

**Answer the questions on the Revision Checklist to evaluate the first
draft you wrote for Exercise 7.**

Check your answers on page 211.

■ Editing

PREWRITING	DRAFTING	REVISING	EDITING	FINAL DRAFT

The last stage of the writing process is editing. When you **edit**, you find and correct mistakes in grammar, mechanics, and usage. Edit the revised draft of "Take It Off!" on page 29. Find and correct the five errors in the essay. Then check your answers on page 212.

Were you able to find all the errors? If you're like most student writers, you need to review grammar, mechanics, and usage. Part II of this book explains the areas that most often trouble student writers. When you need help with a point of grammar, look it up in the table of contents. It will tell you what page or pages of Part II you should read.

The book also gives you a chance to do a more thorough review. If you do the Editing Exercise in this and the next six chapters, you'll review six major areas: nouns, pronouns, verbs, adjectives and adverbs, sentence structure, and punctuation.

Editing Exercise: Nouns

Underline and correct the noun error in each sentence.

Dear Reba,

I received your letter in this mornings mail. It certainly brightened this chilly monday. It's always great to hear from my favorite Aunt.

We've had an unusually cold Fall this year. An early september frost took us by surprise. Most peoples gardens were ruined. You should have seen my poor tomatos! On the other hand, the leafs are especially colorful this year.

Bo and Nedra are really looking forward to halloween. Kids costumes were on sale at the dimestore, so I bought new ghost outfits. This year, we're going trick-or-treating with a few other familys. It will be easier on me and more fun for the childrens.

Well, it's getting late and I have to pack tomorrow's lunchs, so I'll sign off for now. Please give our love to uncle Dan.

Love,

Check your answers on page 212.

CHAPTER 3 | DESCRIBING

The notice above describes a family's pet dog. You've probably seen a notice like it hanging in a store or on a lamp post. The notice contains a good and complete description. The owner wants to make sure that people will recognize the dog.

Skill in describing comes in handy. In this chapter, you'll learn how to write good descriptions.

AFTER WORKING THROUGH THIS CHAPTER, YOU SHOULD BE ABLE TO

▶ IDENTIFY THE OVERALL IMPRESSION OF A DESCRIPTION

▶ USE SPECIFIC DESCRIPTIVE DETAILS

▶ ORGANIZE DESCRIPTIVE DETAILS USING SPACE ORDER

▶ PREWRITE, DRAFT, REVISE, AND EDIT YOUR OWN DESCRIPTION

■ Elements of Descriptive Essays

Reread the notice at the beginning of this chapter. Like all good descriptions, it contains three key elements. It gives readers a clear overall impression. It includes many specific details. And it's organized in a way that makes it easy to picture what's being described.

Main Idea: Overall Impression

Can you picture the dog described at the beginning of this chapter? What's your overall impression of the dog? Do you imagine a funny-looking mutt that's loved by its family? That **overall impression** is the main idea of the description. Every descriptive detail helps create one main picture and feeling in your mind.

Often, the overall impression of a description is stated in a main idea sentence. The sentence is usually included in the introduction to the description. Read this excerpt, or part, of a descriptive essay about a car. The main idea is underlined.

> For more than two years, my brother Jerry has been saving to buy a car. Last week, he finally bought it. The car is quite a beauty. <u>In fact, it's one of the flashiest cars you'll ever see.</u>
>
> Outside, the car is bright red with polished trim. The roof slopes back, and the bottom rides low to the ground. The whole car has a fast, sleek look. It's the kind of car that makes police officers pull out their radar guns.
>
> Inside, you'll find black bucket seats. The dashboard has so many lights and instruments that it looks like a spacecraft's. The instruments show the world that this is a high-performance car.

The main idea sentence gives you the writer's overall impression: the car his brother bought is flashy. The body explains what the writer means. Each supporting detail shows that it is, indeed, a flashy car.

WITH A PARTNER

Look for descriptions of cars in dealers' booklets or in magazines. Read the descriptions carefully. Together, decide on the overall impression the writers want to give you of each car.

Exercise 1

Read the description. Then circle the letter of the sentence that describes the overall impression the description creates.

Description 1

My friend's newborn was as wrinkled as a prune. Its head was funny-shaped. Its face was scratched and had red splotches all over it. Its eyes and mouth were all scrunched up. It held its fists shut tightly while its scrawny legs kicked. But then I realized it was my best buddy's baby. Suddenly, the baby became a beautiful little human being.

(a) The baby was the most beautiful newborn I'd ever seen.

(b) At first, the baby looked ugly and wrinkled.

Description 2

You can recognize our house easily. That's because it's the coziest-looking home on the block. From the street, you walk up a flat stone path to the screened-in porch, with its swing. The house is painted gray with white shutters. Each window has a flowerbox filled with petunias. Outside the front door is a mat that says "Welcome."

(a) The house looks old and run-down.

(b) The house is homey and old-fashioned.

Description 3

My favorite fishing lake is in the backwoods of Georgia. Sitting on its shore, I look out onto the most peaceful scene. Toward the left, a narrow inlet cuts back into the deep green pine forest. Into the middle of the lake juts a large headland. Its red rock bluffs rise up from the deep blue water. Off to the right, the lake reflects forested hills. These highlands stretch back as far as the eye can see. I'd visit the lake even if the fishing were awful.

(a) The lake is beautiful and peaceful.

(b) The lake has a narrow inlet on the left.

Check your answers on page 212.

Developing the Main Idea: Descriptive Details

How does a writer create a picture in the reader's mind? The writer uses **descriptive details**. To be descriptive, a detail must appeal to one of the five senses: sight, hearing, taste, smell, or touch. In other words, a descriptive detail must help you imagine how something looks, sounds, tastes, smells, or feels.

"Sight words" are especially important in a description. Sight words name the color, size, or shape of something. For example, look back at the lost-dog notice at the beginning of this chapter. These words help you "see" the dog in your mind:

▶ graying muzzle   ▶ long, fine hair

▶ one blue eye, one brown   ▶ short legs

▶ brown, pointed ears   ▶ long, crooked tail

▶ brown and silver spotted

Now, look back at the paragraph about Jerry's new car, on page 32. What words and phrases help you picture it? You probably chose these:

▶ bright red   ▶ fast

▶ polished trim   ▶ sleek

▶ sloped roof   ▶ black bucket seats

▶ low to the ground   ▶ dashboard . . . like a spacecraft's

In the cases of the dog and the car, describing looks is important. As a result, the two descriptions appeal to the sense of sight. But in other cases, a writer might appeal to a different sense or senses.

For example, what if you were describing dinner at an Italian restaurant? You might describe the aroma of oregano and tomatoes. You might describe the spicy flavor of Italian sausage. Or you might describe the crunch of the bread and the sting of the hot cheese as you bite into them.

When you write a description, think about the sense or senses you should appeal to. Make your readers see, hear, taste, smell, or feel what you're describing.

IN YOUR JOURNAL

Draw six lines down a page to make five columns. At the top of each column, write one of the five senses: sight, hearing, taste, smell, touch. Visit or recall a visit to a crowded fast-food restaurant. Brainstorm about the sights, sounds, tastes, smells, and feelings. Write down as many descriptive details for each of the senses as you can.

Exercise 2

Complete the paragraph by adding descriptive details.

Each spring when I was a child, a traveling carnival would come to town. I loved

visiting it. My favorite ride was the _____ . If I close my

eyes, I can still picture it. It was _____

_____

_____

_____ .

What did it feel like to be on the ride? It was _____

_____

_____

_____

Food stands filled the air with tempting aromas:_____

_____

_____

_____

I always bought _____ to eat. It tasted _____

_____

_____

_____

As I walked, I could hear the sounds of_____

_____

_____

_____

Answers will vary.

Organizing Ideas: Space Order

Think of a jigsaw puzzle. Its pieces contain all the details to create a whole picture. But if the pieces are placed in the wrong order, they create nothing but a jumble.

The same is true of descriptive details in an essay. If you aren't careful about how you organize them, you'll create a jumble. Your reader will have a hard time picturing what you're describing. But if you follow space order, you'll create a complete picture. When you put details in **space order**, you organize them in the order that you see or experience them.

Suppose you're describing a party. Each detail describes a group of people in the room. Help your reader picture the scene by ordering the details **from left to right**. Write as if your eyes were moving from left to right through the room:

Main Idea   ⟶   The party looked like a lot of fun.

Detail 1   ⟶   On the left was . . .

Detail 2   ⟶   In the middle was . . .

Detail 3   ⟶   On the right was . . .

The description of the Georgia lake, on page 33, is organized from left to right.

Space order can also be **from top to bottom** or **from head to toe** (or tail). That's the order the dog owner followed in the description of the dog.

Sometimes, space order is **from outside to inside**. That's the order the brother used to describe Jerry's new car. Another way of describing is **from far away to close up**. The description of the house, on page 33, is organized this way.

Naturally, if you need to, you can reverse any of the orders—from close up to far away, from inside to outside, and so on.

WITH A PARTNER

Write a short description of something without naming it. Give your description to someone else. See if he or she can guess what it is. Then switch roles. Read your partner's description and try to guess what he or she is describing.

Exercise 3

Tell how each paragraph is organized—from left to right, from outside to inside, or from far away to close up.

1. The heart-shaped box was beautiful. It was covered in bright red satin adorned with golden lace. In gold letters on the lid it said, "To My Darling." I lifted the lid, and there were a dozen hand-dipped chocolates. Each was nestled in its own doily.

   Order: _____

2. From the plane, the countryside looked like a patchwork quilt. Cars the size of ants crawled down roads no wider than ribbons. As we began to descend, my point of view changed. The patches became cornfields. The ant-like cars grew bigger as the roads grew wider.

   Order: _____

3. It was the messiest room I'd ever seen. To my left was an unmade bed. Sheets and blankets lay knotted on top of it. In the middle of the floor was a cardboard pizza box. It was smeared with grease and littered with half-chewed crusts. To my right was a mountain of dirty jeans and T-shirts.

   Order: _____

Check your answers on page 212.

IN YOUR JOURNAL

Write a description of your favorite room in your home. Be sure to include plenty of sight words. Use space order to organize the details in your description. Describe the room from left to right.

■ Read a Descriptive Essay

You've studied three elements of description: overall impressions, descriptive details, and space order. Look for these elements as you read the following descriptive essay.

In this essay, a young writer describes one of her favorite spots—a beach in North Carolina. As you read the description, picture what it's like to run on the beach. Try to see and feel what she saw and felt.

Running on the Beach

by Leah Kohlenberg

(1) Since moving to North Carolina a year ago, I have discovered the simple pleasure of running on the beach.

(2) From May to September, a runner has to brave 90-degree temperatures. She has to share the beach with the **hordes**[1] of tourists, sun worshippers, and surfers that flock there.

(3) But come October, the winds begin to pick up. The water chills. The sun seems to hang higher in the sky, with its heat further out of reach. The beach clears out except for a few fishermen and **beachcombers**[2]. That is when I head down narrow streets to a **boardwalk**[3] built parallel to the Atlantic Ocean's shores.

(4) The boardwalk is like a ghost town. I walk past fast-food stands with boarded windows. In faded colors, a sign advertises burgers and fries, snow cones, and ice cream. The sweet aroma of caramel corn that I remember from the summer has been replaced by the sharp, salty smell of the ocean.

(5) There are wooden walkways built from the boardwalk to the edge of the sand. I cannot see the beach at first. But as I walk along the wooden planks, the clear, cloudless sky gives way at the horizon to the deeper blue of the water.

---

[1] **hordes:** large crowds
[2] **beachcombers:** people who search the beach for seashells or other items
[3] **boardwalk:** walkway

(6) The roar and crash of the waves draws me to the water's edge. The waves roll in. They push their white-foamed edges ahead, driving the foam into the sand. The foam hisses like bacon frying.

(7) The air is cool as I walk back up to the top of the beach. My sneakers sink into the sand. A dark wooden pier juts out from the shore to my right. From this distance, it looks as if it has been constructed of sticks by a child's hand. I decide that I will run to the pier and slap my hand against one of its supports.

(8) Running on the beach is not really running at all. A head wind gently pushes against me. The sand clutches at my feet so that I grind my way along. It is like running in a dream.

(9) I fall into a rhythm. My breath is coming deeper. My legs are churning. I look up and the pier seems to have more than doubled in size.

(10) Up ahead, fishermen sit in folding chairs. Knee-high boots stand beside the chairs. Fishing poles have been driven into the sand.

(11) I see a family walking under the pier that now **looms**[4] ahead. Two small children play tag with the waves. They dart away, squealing, as the water reaches out toward them and then retreats.

(12) With the wind behind me, it is as if I have been let loose from a harness. I pick up the pace.

(13) I fly past the fishermen, ducking under their lines. Some of them wake from their **stupor**[5] and yell at me, but I am already gone.

(14) A few hundred yards more and my muscles start to go weak. I have to think about breathing deeply. My shirt is damp with sweat, and the air feels cool against my skin.

(15) I come over a ridge, and there it is: my finish line. My footprints remain clear in the sand from the walkway to the water's edge. I cross with a final burst. The wood of the pier is damp and rough.

(16) My breath begins to slow until it matches the rhythm of the waves. They roll in and back as I breathe the cool, clean-smelling air in time. The sun, so high in the sky, glistens off the water.

(17) It is in this quiet moment that I realize why this is my favorite place to run.

---

[4] **looms:** seems to appear before one's eyes
[5] **stupor:** daze

Check Your Understanding

PART A

Circle the answer to each question about "Running on the Beach." Look back at the essay if you need to.

1. What is the writer's overall impression of running on the beach?
   (a) It's hard work but good for a person's health.
   (b) The almost-deserted beach is a beautiful place to run.

2. What senses does the writer appeal to in paragraph 4?
   (a) sight and smell
   (b) hearing and touch

3. What senses does the writer appeal to in paragraph 6?
   (a) sound and sight
   (b) touch and smell

4. The writer describes what it's like to run to a pier. How does she organize the description?
   (a) from top to bottom
   (b) from far away to close up

PART B

For each of the following senses, list at least two descriptive details included in the essay.

1. sight: _____

   _____

2. sound: _____

   _____

3. smell: _____

   _____

4. touch: _____

   _____

Check your answers on page 212.

■ Write a Descriptive Essay

Prewriting: Selecting a Topic and Purpose

In "Running on the Beach," Leah Kohlenberg describes a place that is special to her. **Write a descriptive essay about a place or person that's special to you.** Your purpose is to describe. The topic you choose to describe could be

- ▶ A landscape, or outdoor scene
- ▶ A prized possession
- ▶ Another person
- ▶ Yourself

Below are some ideas to help you get started. Choose *one* of these topics or use one of your own. You may also want to check your journal. See if you have written about something or someone that you would enjoy describing in an essay.

- ▶ A private place where you go when you need to be alone
- ▶ An exciting place, such as an amusement park
- ▶ A relaxing place, such as a lake
- ▶ Something special you own, such as a car or a ring
- ▶ Your husband or wife, boyfriend or girlfriend
- ▶ Your child
- ▶ What you see when you look in the mirror

Write your topic below.

Topic: _____

Prewriting: Developing Your Topic

Now that you have your topic, you need to think of details to develop it. One excellent way to think of descriptive details is to observe the person or thing you're describing. **Observing** is a special kind of brainstorming.

When you observe, you look at your subject from every angle. You note details like color and size and shape. You also think of how your subject involves your other senses, such as touch or smell. Then you list each detail.

Here are the notes a student wrote. The topic of his description was the view he saw from his front porch.

<u>Sights</u>	<u>Sounds</u>	<u>Smells</u>
white frame house	honking horns	stink of diesel
brown brick factory	squealing brakes	fumes
smokestacks	blaring car radios	
skyscrapers		
steel and glass		

Carefully observe the person or thing you chose to describe. If you can't observe your subject, picture it (or him or her) in your mind.

On the lines below, make an observation chart like the one above. Write down as many descriptive details as you can.

_____

_____

_____

_____

_____

_____

_____

_____

_____

Prewriting: Organizing Your Ideas

Finish prewriting by organizing your ideas.

▶ **Write a main idea sentence.**

Ask yourself, What overall impression do my descriptive details make?

Main idea sentence: _____

_____

▶ **Now, group your descriptive details.**

Decide if you need one, two, or more paragraphs for the body of your essay. Draw a line around the details that go together in each paragraph. Or, if you prefer, draw clusters showing how the details go together.

▶ **Decide what order to put your details in.**

Do you want to describe a person from head to toe? An object from the outside to the inside? A place from left to right or from far away to close up?

The student who made the observation chart chose to organize his details from close up to far away. What kind of order will you use? **Write the order below.**

Order: _____

Many writers also find it helpful to draw a sketch of the space order they plan to use. Try drawing one if you wish. Follow the student's example.

My neighborhood   factories   skyscrapers

Drafting

The next stage of the writing process is drafting. During this stage, you use your prewriting plan to write. Remember that a first draft is just a first try. You'll have a chance to improve your writing when you revise and edit.

Using your plan, write a first draft on the topic of your choice. If you need more space, write on another piece of paper.

WRITE AN
INTRODUCTION.
INCLUDE A
MAIN IDEA
SENTENCE.

_____

_____

_____

_____

_____

_____

_____

USE
DESCRIPTIVE
DETAILS IN
THE BODY.

_____

_____

_____

_____

_____

_____

_____

WRITE A
CONCLUSION
THAT
RESTATES
THE MAIN
IDEA.

_____

_____

_____

Revising

The next stage is to evaluate your first draft, alone or with a partner. First, do the Revision Warm-Up. Then use the Revision Checklist to revise your draft.

Revision Warm-Up

Evaluate the student's first draft by answering each question on the Revision Checklist.

The View from My Front Porch

After a long, hot day at work, I like to sit on my front porch with something cool to drink.

White frame houses line my block. We moved to our home last summer. Horns honk, bus brakes squeal, and the diesel fumes stink. But then the neighborhood quiets down. The brown brick walls of factories rise several stories above the homes. Smokestacks rise even higher above the factory roofs. Smoke swirls out of one. It rises from another. The downtown skyscrapers line up along the horizon. These glass and steel giants create the city's skyline. Their windows reflect the sun's golden setting rays.

Soon, thousands of small white city lights will replace the day, and the kids will drive by with their radios blaring.

☑ Revision Checklist

Yes	No	
☐	☐	**1.** Does the essay have an introductory paragraph or paragraphs?
☐	☐	**2.** Is the overall impression stated in a main idea sentence in the introduction?
☐	☐	**3.** Does the body contain at least one paragraph?
☐	☐	**4.** Do all the descriptive details support the overall impression?
☐	☐	**5.** Does the body contain enough descriptive details to develop the overall impression?
☐	☐	**6.** Are the details in the body arranged in a logical space order?
☐	☐	**7.** Is there a paragraph or paragraphs of conclusion?
☐	☐	**8.** Does the conclusion help sum up the overall impression?
☐	☐	**9.** Are all the sentences and ideas clear?

Check your answers on page 213.

Editing

The last stage of the writing process is editing. During this stage, you look for and correct errors in grammar, mechanics, and usage.

Do the Editing Exercise. Then look for and correct any noun and pronoun errors as well as other errors in your draft. If possible, work with a partner.

Editing Exercise: Pronouns

Underline and correct the nine pronoun errors in the letter.

Dear Linn,

Its too bad you couldn't make it to our New Year's Eve party. Glenn and myself missed having you.

About twenty of our friends showed up. As usual, the Nielands brought they're kids. I usually love children, but the Nieland kids are so loud! They gave Glenn and I a headache. The Smiths sort of invited theirselves. However, we didn't really mind. We enjoyed having them.

We decorated the living room with the silver streamers and balloons that you gave to we. Glenn and me put the long table on the right side of the living room. It was loaded with all kinds of food. Everyone loved Glenn's version of potato salad. Mine's was less popular. However, them pizza puffs I made were gobbled up fast.

We're already beginning to plan next year's party, and we hope you can come. Put it on your calendar now!

Love,

Juanita

Check your answers on page 213.

Chapter 4 | NARRATING

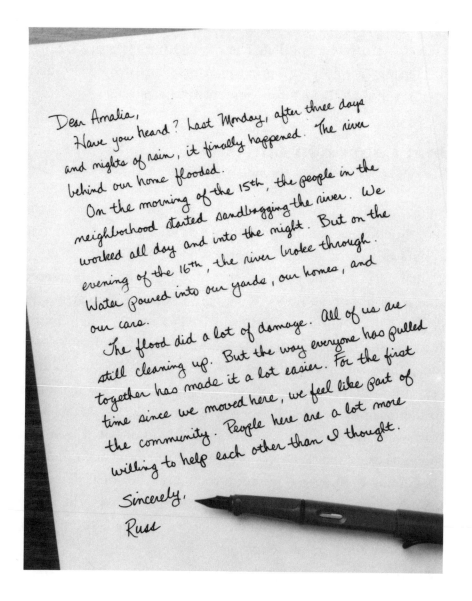

Dear Amalia,

Have you heard? Last Monday, after three days and nights of rain, it finally happened. The river behind our home flooded.

On the morning of the 15th, the people in the neighborhood started sandbagging the river. We worked all day and into the night. But on the evening of the 16th, the river broke through. Water poured into our yards, our homes, and our cars.

The flood did a lot of damage. All of us are still cleaning up. But the way everyone has pulled together has made it a lot easier. For the first time since we moved here, we feel like part of the community. People here are a lot more willing to help each other than I thought.

Sincerely,
Russ

The letter above is a **personal narrative**—the story of a person's experiences. Personal narratives are a familiar kind of writing. In fact, you've already written one if you've ever composed a letter about a family event or a postcard about a trip. In this chapter, you'll learn more about writing narratives.

AFTER WORKING THROUGH THIS CHAPTER, YOU SHOULD BE ABLE TO
▶ FIND THE MAIN IDEA OF A PERSONAL NARRATIVE
▶ IDENTIFY THREE KINDS OF CONFLICTS
▶ USE TIME ORDER TO ORGANIZE IDEAS
▶ PREWRITE, DRAFT, REVISE, AND EDIT A PERSONAL NARRATIVE

■ Elements of Personal Narratives

In many ways, the letter at the beginning of this chapter is a typical personal narrative. It tells the story of a conflict. The meaning of the story is summed up at the end. And the story is told in the order in which it happened. In this section, you'll take a closer look at these three elements of narration.

Main Idea: Lesson in Life

Personal experience often teaches us. Many times, people learn a lesson in life when something unusual happens to them. For example, they may change their attitude toward a person or situation. Or they may discover something about themselves, about others, or about the world. This lesson in life is very often the main idea of a narrative. It is the point the writer wants to make about an experience.

Reread the letter about the flood. What is the point of the narrative? If you're not sure, ask yourself, What did the writer learn as a result of fighting the flood? The writer learned that his neighbors were more willing to help than he'd thought.

Where does the writer make this statement? He sums up this point in the last few sentences of his letter. Personal narratives often end with a main idea sentence. Wrapping up the meaning of what happened is a good way to conclude a story.

That is one way that personal narratives are a little different from other kinds of essays. You've learned that it's a good idea to write your main idea statement right at the beginning of an essay, in the introduction. Personal narratives, however, sometimes save the main idea for last. In many cases, the writer uses the first few sentences of the essay to "set the stage." That means the writer describes the situation in which the personal experience took place.

For example, look again at the letter at the beginning of this chapter. The first paragraph sets the stage by letting you know that a flood occurred. The flood is the situation in which the writer learned the truth about his neighbors.

IN YOUR JOURNAL

Each of the following sayings could be the main idea of a narrative. Select one saying, and write a story to go along with it. Make the saying the last sentence of your story.

▶ Look before you leap.
▶ You can't judge a book by its cover.
▶ Absence makes the heart grow fonder.

Exercise 1

PART A

Underline the main idea sentence of each personal narrative.

1. We'd heard the tornado watch announced on the radio. But we didn't pay much attention to it. Then, we noticed the funnel cloud way off on the hill. Lisa and I grabbed the kids and headed for the basement. At first, it sounded as if a huge train were bearing down on us. Then, the swirling winds hit. Smash! Within seconds, our house was destroyed. I was in shock. All that we'd worked for was gone. Yet I thanked God we were alive. As I hugged my wife and kids, I was reminded of what really matters to me.

2. Three killings in our neighborhood proved the gangs had gotten out of hand. One of the dead was a two-year-old girl. That's when some neighborhood people decided to fight back. One night we gathered together in the office of our alderman. We decided to "take back the streets." From then on, everyone would leave his or her porch lights on. We'd stay outside as much as possible. If we saw any criminal act, we'd contact the police. And we'd cooperate with them. We would prove that people working together can get rid of gangs.

PART B

Circle the letter of the best main idea sentence to end this narrative.

There I stood—at the edge of the pool. Everyone else was enjoying the cool water on this hot day. But I was scared. I had been afraid of water all my life. Now, however, I was determined to overcome that fear. I held my nose, shut my eyes, and jumped. At first, the water closing over my head terrified me. But soon, my feet touched bottom. I quickly pushed myself up. When I reached the surface, I grabbed the edge of the pool and floated. I had done it!

(a) I had stood at the edge of the pool and jumped in.

(b) I realized then that it's foolish to let fear rule your life.

Check your answers on page 213.

Developing the Main Idea: Conflict

Often, people learn a lesson in life when they go through some kind of **conflict**—a problem or struggle. For that reason, many personal narratives tell the story of a conflict. Conflict captures and holds people's interest. Think of a TV show or movie that you recently saw and liked. What problems did the people face? Did you wonder how the people would solve them? Conflict builds suspense in viewers' (and readers') minds. It makes them wonder what will happen next.

The three main kinds of conflicts are **person against person**, **person against nature**, and **person against himself or herself**. If you understand the three kinds of conflict, you'll become a better reader as well as writer of narratives.

Person Against Person This kind of conflict happens when people disagree or compete with each other. For example, an argument between a husband and wife is a person-against-person conflict. So is tension between salespeople trying to outsell each other to earn a bonus.

Person Against Nature This kind of conflict involves problems caused by natural disasters. The letter at the beginning of this chapter is about a person-against-nature conflict: neighbors fighting a flood. Fires, storms, and disease are other examples of natural disasters that can cause person-against-nature conflicts.

Person Against Self This kind of conflict involves a struggle within a person. For example, a woman who is torn between having children or having a career is in a person-against-self conflict. So is a man who is struggling to break a gambling habit.

WITH A PARTNER

Skim the front page of a newspaper. Read the headlines and the first paragraph of each story. How many stories involve conflict? Together, decide which kind of conflict is described in each story.

Exercise 2

PART A

Match each example with the correct kind of conflict.

_____ **1.** the Bears against the Lions   **(a)** person against person

_____ **2.** a woman trying not to drink   **(b)** person against nature

_____ **3.** a pilot landing in thick fog   **(c)** person against self

PART B

Write the name of the kind of conflict each paragraph is about.

1. I didn't know what to do. On the one hand, I knew I'd be happier living apart from Al. On the other, I couldn't bear to separate the kids from their dad.

_____

2. Thank God it was over. It had been a tough fire to fight. The freezing weather had made it even tougher. Two men were badly hurt.

_____

3. I'd gone almost twenty-four hours without sleep. My boss had given me yet another impossible deadline. I was doing the best I could. But once again, it wasn't good enough for him. When he walked over and asked for the report, I wearily told him I wasn't finished writing it. "That's it!" he roared. "You're fired!" Angrily, I replied, "You can't fire me, because I quit!"

_____

Check your answers on page 213.

IN YOUR JOURNAL

Think about conflicts that you've faced in your life. Make three brainstorming lists—one for each kind of conflict. Then, list as many conflicts as you can for each.

Organizing Ideas: Time Order

When you tell a story, you usually tell the events in the order in which they happened. You begin by talking about what happened first, then what happened next, and so on. This organization of ideas is called **time order**. Time order is an excellent way to organize a personal narrative.

For example, read the following paragraph, which is *not* written in time order. Ask yourself if it is easy to understand what happened.

> The day that I graduated, everything seemed to go wrong. On our way to school, our car got a flat tire. We ended up arriving ten minutes after the ceremony had started. When I went to pick up my suit, the cleaners couldn't find it. I had to borrow my brother's suit, which was too big. I woke up with a sore throat and fever. Worst of all, I tripped as I walked across the stage.

All the events are included in the paragraph. However, the story is difficult to follow. That's because the events are not in the order in which they occurred. See what happens when the narrative is written in time order.

> The day that I graduated, everything seemed to go wrong. First, I woke up with a sore throat and fever. Then, when I went to pick up my suit, the cleaners couldn't find it. I ended up having to borrow my brother's suit, which was too big. On our way to school, our car got a flat tire. We ended up arriving ten minutes after the ceremony had started. Last but not least, I tripped as I walked across the stage.

As you can see, organizing the story in time order makes it easy to follow.

IN YOUR JOURNAL

Describe an exciting play from a recent sporting event. Tell about the play in detail. Put the actions in time order.

Exercise 3

....

**Put each list of events in time order. Number the first event 1, the
second event 2, and so on.**

1. _____ The doctor told me I had diabetes.

 _____ I had to go through tests to see what was wrong.

 _____ I hadn't been feeling right for months.

 _____ I decided to go see the doctor.

 _____ By watching my diet and taking shots, I feel great.

2. _____ All ten pins fell—a strike!

 _____ I had to get a strike to beat my old bowling rival.

 _____ The ball crashed into the lead pin.

 _____ The ball rolled down the lane.

 _____ I swung my arm forward and let the ball fly.

3. _____ The agency worker gave me a list of job openings.

 _____ I found a position as a sales associate.

 _____ I went to our city's employment office.

 _____ I was laid off from my job.

4. _____ I went to the station to identify the suspect.

 _____ I heard footsteps on my front porch late at night.

 _____ The police chased a prowler through my backyard.

 _____ I called the police.

 _____ The officers cornered and caught the prowler.

Check your answers on page 213.

Read a Personal Narrative

You've studied three elements of personal narratives: the lesson-in-life main idea, conflict, and time order. Look for these elements as you read the following narrative.

A United States in which all people have equal rights—that was the dream of African-American leader Malcolm X. As a child, Malcolm X experienced many forms of racism. In "Mr. Ostrowski," he tells the story of an experience that changed his life.

Mr. Ostrowski

from *The Autobiography of Malcolm X*
by Malcolm X as told to Alex Haley

My restlessness with **Mason**[1]—and for the first time in my life a restlessness with being around white people—began as soon as I got back home and entered eighth grade. . . .

Somehow, I happened to be alone in the classroom with Mr. Ostrowski, my English teacher. He was a tall, rather reddish white man and he had a thick mustache. I had gotten some of my best **marks**[2] under him, and he had always made me feel that he liked me. He was, as I have mentioned, a natural-born "advisor," about what you ought to read, to do, or think—about any and everything. We used to make unkind jokes about him: why was he teaching in Mason instead of somewhere else, getting for himself some of the "success in life" that he kept telling us how to get?

I know that he probably meant well in what he happened to advise me that day. I doubt that he meant any harm. It was just in his nature as an American white man. I was one of his top students, and one of the school's top students—but all he could see for me was the kind of future "in your place" that almost all white people see for black people.

---

[1] **Mason:** Michigan town where Malcolm X went to junior high
[2] **marks:** grades

He told me, "Malcolm, you ought to be thinking about a career. Have you been giving it thought?"

The truth is, I hadn't. I never have figured out why I told him, "Well, yes, sir, I've been thinking I'd like to be a lawyer." **Lansing**[3] certainly had no Negro lawyers—or doctors either—in those days, to hold up an image I might have **aspired**[4] to. All I really knew for certain was that a lawyer didn't wash dishes, as I was doing.

Mr. Ostrowski looked surprised, I remember, and leaned back in his chair and clasped his hands behind his head. He kind of half-smiled and said, "Malcolm, one of life's first needs is for us to be realistic. Don't misunderstand me, now. We all here like you, you know that. But you've got to be realistic about being a nigger. A lawyer—that's no realistic goal for a nigger. You need to think about something you *can* be. You're good with your hands—making things. Everybody admires your carpentry shop work. Why don't you plan on carpentry? People like you as a person—you'd get all kinds of work."

The more I thought afterwards about what he said, the more uneasy it made me. It just kept treading around in my mind.

What made it really begin to disturb me was Mr. Ostrowski's advice to others in my class—all of them white. Most of them had told him they were planning to become farmers. But those who wanted to strike out on their own, to try something new, he had encouraged. Some, mostly girls, wanted to be teachers. A few wanted other professions, such as one boy who wanted to become a county agent; another, a veterinarian; and one girl wanted to be a nurse. They all reported that Mr. Ostrowski had encouraged what they had wanted. Yet nearly none of them had earned marks equal to mine.

It was a surprising thing that I had never thought of it that way before, but I realized that whatever I wasn't, I *was* smarter than nearly all of those white kids. But apparently I was still not intelligent enough, in their eyes, to become whatever *I* wanted to be.

It was then that I began to change—inside.

••

---

[3] **Lansing:** Michigan city where Malcolm X grew up
[4] **aspired:** hoped to live up to

Check Your Understanding

PART A

Answer each question about "Mr. Ostrowski." Look back at the essay if you need to.

1. What kind of conflict takes place in "Mr. Ostrowski"? Circle the letter.

    (a) person against person

    (b) person against nature

    (c) person against self

2. What is the main idea of the essay? Circle the letter.

    (a) Malcolm X realized he wasn't smart enough to be a lawyer.

    (b) Malcolm X learned to pick realistic career goals.

    (c) Malcolm X discovered his teacher had racist attitudes.

3. In what order do the following events take place? Number the first event 1, the second event 2, and so on.

    _____ Malcolm X says he'd like to be a lawyer.

    _____ Malcolm X finds himself alone with his English teacher.

    _____ Mr. Ostrowski tells Malcolm X he should be a carpenter.

    _____ Malcolm X realizes Mr. Ostrowski treats whites differently from blacks.

    _____ Mr. Ostrowski asks about Malcolm X's career plans.

PART B

Answer each question in a sentence or two.

1. Where in the narrative does Malcolm X "set the stage" for the conflict?

    _____

    _____

2. Malcolm X says that he "began to change—inside" after his meeting with Mr. Ostrowski. What change do you think Malcolm X underwent?

    _____

    _____

Check your answers on page 214.

■ | Write a Personal Narrative

Prewriting: Selecting a Topic and Purpose

In "Mr. Ostrowski," Malcolm X talks about a conflict he experienced. As a result of the conflict, he discovered something about the world and the people around him. **Write your own personal narrative. Write about a conflict that you experienced. Choose a conflict that taught you something.** Your purpose is to tell the story of the conflict. The conflict you choose to describe could be

- ▶ Between you and another person or other people
- ▶ Caused by a natural disaster
- ▶ Experienced within yourself

Below are some ideas to help you get started. Choose *one* of these topics or use one of your own. You may also want to check your journal. See if you have written about something or someone that you would enjoy describing in an essay. Don't forget to include descriptive details to help your readers picture events.

- ▶ An argument with your husband or wife
- ▶ A problem with your boss
- ▶ A sports competition
- ▶ An illness from which you've recovered
- ▶ A bad habit you've struggled to break
- ▶ A difficult choice you've had to make
- ▶ A fear you've overcome

Write your topic below.

Topic:_____

Prewriting: Developing Your Topic

Now that you have your topic, you need to think of details to develop it. Questioning is a good way to get ideas for a personal narrative. (You learned about questioning in Chapter 2.)

Here's how a student used questioning to develop ideas. Her topic was overcoming a fear of flying.

Who? _Me and my friend Carlos_

What? _Went for a plane ride_

Where? _In Carlos's plane in the sky over my hometown_

When? _Last month_

Why? _Overcame my fear of flying, was missing out on a promotion_

How? _Pictured myself on the ground, victorious; took deep breaths; relaxed; looked around and began to enjoy myself_

On the lines below, list ideas to develop your topic. Follow the student example and use questioning. Or, if you prefer, use a different method, such as brainstorming or freewriting.

_____

_____

_____

_____

_____

_____

_____

_____

_____

_____

Prewriting: Organizing Your Ideas

Finish prewriting by organizing your ideas.

▶ **Write a main idea sentence.**

Ask yourself, What did I learn as a result of the conflict I'm writing about?

Main idea sentence: _____

_____

▶ **Now, group your supporting details.**

Decide if you need one, two, or more paragraphs for the body of your essay. Draw a line around the details that go together in each paragraph. Or, if you prefer, draw clusters showing how the details go together.

▶ **Put your supporting details in time order.**

An easy way to do this is to number each paragraph and each detail within the paragraph. If you wish, follow the student's example.

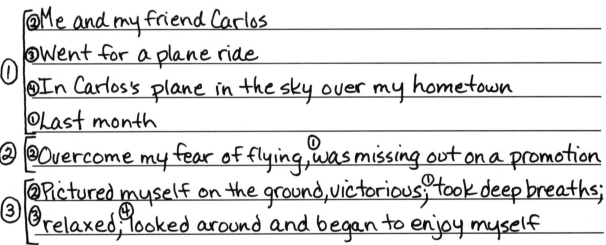

① ② Me and my friend Carlos
③ Went for a plane ride
④ In Carlos's plane in the sky over my hometown
① Last month

② ② Overcome my fear of flying, ① was missing out on a promotion

③ ② Pictured myself on the ground, victorious; ① took deep breaths; ③ relaxed; ④ looked around and began to enjoy myself

Drafting

The next stage of the writing process is drafting. During this step, you use your prewriting plan to write. Remember that a first draft is just a first try. You'll have a chance to improve your writing when you revise and edit.

Using your plan, write a first draft on the topic of your choice. If you need more space, write on another piece of paper.

BEGIN BY
SETTING THE
STAGE.

_____

_____

_____

_____

_____

WRITE YOUR
STORY IN
TIME ORDER.

_____

_____

_____

_____

USE
DESCRIPTIVE
DETAILS.

_____

_____

_____

_____

_____

_____

CONCLUDE
WITH THE
MAIN IDEA.

_____

_____

Revising

The next stage is to evaluate your first draft, alone or with a partner. First, do the Revision Warm-Up. Then use the Revision Checklist to revise your draft.

Revision Warm-Up

Follow the directions to revise the essay below.

1. In the first paragraph is a sentence that doesn't belong. Draw a line through it.

2. Add descriptive details to paragraph 3. What amazing sights did the writer see?

3. The conclusion doesn't have a main idea sentence. Add one or two.

Sky High

Last month, I found myself in a place I'd never been before. I was high over my hometown in a small plane piloted by my friend Carlos. Carlos and I went to grade school together. I was terrified. My heart was pounding loudly in my ears, and I had closed my eyes so tightly that my forehead hurt. How did I get myself into this? I wondered.

Actually, I knew very well. My fear of flying was keeping me from a promotion. I was trying to overcome my fear.

"Are you OK?" Carlos asked. "I guess so," I said. But I was so scared that I was having trouble talking. Would I faint? I took a deep breath. Then, I pictured myself on the ground, victorious. The thought made me relax. Slowly, I opened one eye, then the other. I looked out the window and saw the most amazing sights. To my surprise, I began to enjoy myself.

In no time at all, Carlos said, "We're landing." As I left the plane, my knees were wobbly but my head was clear.

Check your answers on page 214.

☞ Revision Checklist

Yes	No	
☐	☐	**1.** Does the introductory paragraph or paragraphs set the stage?
☐	☐	**2.** Are the events in the body in time order?
☐	☐	**3.** Are there enough descriptive details to help you picture the events?
☐	☐	**4.** Are there details or sentences that don't belong?
☐	☐	**5.** Does the conclusion include a main idea sentence?
☐	☐	**6.** Are all the sentences and ideas clear?

Editing

The last stage of the writing process is editing. During this stage, you look for and correct errors in grammar, mechanics, and usage.

Do the Editing Exercise. Then look for and correct any noun, pronoun, and verb errors as well as any other errors in your draft. If possible, work with a partner.

Editing Exercise: Verbs

Underline and correct the seven verb errors in the essay.

Back to School

I was really nervous about going back to school. My husband and kids was all for it. But I wasn't so sure. I hate school when I was a teenager. Would I hate it now? I also was afraid that I was too old for school.

Then, I run into an old friend. She said that she taking high school classes through the library. She said that it was fun. She also said that age don't matter.

Now, my friend and I go to class two mornings a week. I am doing very well. I love school. My husband say he is proud of me. My kids is proud too. I never thought I could do so well.

Check your answers on page 214.

CHAPTER 5 | EXPLAINING HOW

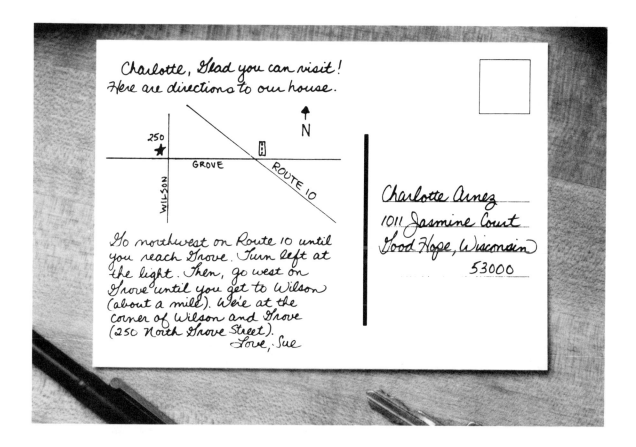

The postcard above explains how to do something—specifically, how to get to a person's home. "How-to" essays have a similar purpose. They, too, explain how to do something. In this chapter, you'll learn what goes into a good how-to essay.

AFTER WORKING THROUGH THIS CHAPTER, YOU SHOULD BE ABLE TO
- ▶ FIND THE MAIN IDEA OF A HOW-TO ESSAY
- ▶ IDENTIFY THE STEPS INVOLVED IN A PROCESS
- ▶ USE TIME ORDER TO ORGANIZE THE STEPS IN A PROCESS
- ▶ PREWRITE, DRAFT, REVISE, AND EDIT YOUR OWN HOW-TO ESSAY

■ Elements of How-To Essays

Reread the postcard at the beginning of this chapter. Though instructions are not an essay, they have some of the same elements as a good how-to. They clearly state a goal. They explain how to reach the goal. And the explanation is easy to follow because it's well organized.

Main Idea: Stating a Goal

When you do something, you usually have a goal in mind. You want to make something, get something, fix something, or achieve something. Reaching that goal is the main idea behind a how-to essay. When you write a how-to, you explain to your readers how to reach a goal.

Usually, the main idea is stated in the introduction of the how-to essay. Sometimes, writers also use the introduction to motivate readers to reach the goal. By describing benefits of following the instructions in the essay, writers can make readers want to follow all the steps.

As you read the following how-to essay, ask yourself, What goal is the writer explaining how to reach? What are the benefits of reaching the goal?

Throw Away Your Fork

If you're not Asian, you may eat your chicken chow mein with a fork. But if you follow these steps, you can learn to eat with chopsticks. It's fun, and it makes the food taste even better!

First, hold a chopstick between your thumb and index finger. Brace the bottom of the stick (the tapered, or more pointed, end) against the top of your fourth finger. Next, hold the other chopstick with your thumb, index finger, and middle finger. That's just the way you would hold a pencil. Now, place the two ends of the chopsticks around a bit of food. Squeeze the two ends together, and you can pick it up.

Next time you eat Chinese food, try using chopsticks. Eating with them takes a little patience, but with practice, you'll get used to it. Before you know it, you'll be ready to throw away your fork!

The main idea of the essay is clearly stated in the introduction. The goal is to learn how to use chopsticks. The benefits of reaching the goal are also clearly stated. According to the writer, eating with chopsticks is fun and makes the food taste even better.

Exercise 1

Read the essay. Underline the main idea sentence in the introduction. Then underline the sentence that states a benefit.

Strike!

Bowling a strike is the aim of every bowler. To reach this goal, you have to deliver the ball properly. Here are the steps a right-handed bowler should take. If you follow them, you'll improve your chance of bowling a strike.

First, you should face the pins, keeping your feet together. Hold the ball slightly above your waist.

Second, step forward on your right foot. As you step, extend your right arm, and then step forward on your left foot. As you step, bring the ball back behind you.

Third, move your right foot forward just as the ball is as far back as your arm can go. Slide your left foot forward, and as you slide, swing the ball down and forward. Finally, stop your slide and release the ball, thumb first. Let your right hand follow forward and up.

Learning these steps takes time and practice. But once you've learned them, you'll become a better bowler.

Check your answers on page 214.

WITH A PARTNER

To get people to buy a product, advertisers show benefits of owning or using it. For example, some TV commercials hint that wearing a particular cologne will make a man more handsome and popular. Here are some other benefits often used to motivate people to buy:

- ▶ Saving time or money
- ▶ Feeling younger or healthier
- ▶ Feeling personal satisfaction
- ▶ Protecting one's family
- ▶ Becoming more skilled
- ▶ Enjoying oneself

Together, analyze some TV or magazine ads. Decide which benefit or benefits are included in each ad.

Developing the Main Idea: Steps in a Process

A how-to essay does more than state a goal. It gives steps that explain how to reach the goal. Together, these steps form a **process**.

Look below at the paragraphs from the essay on bowling. Notice the underlined words. They tell each **step**—each action—that should be taken to bowl a strike.

First, you <u>should face</u> the pins, keeping your feet together. <u>Hold</u> the ball slightly above your waist.

Second, <u>step</u> forward on your right foot. As you step, <u>extend</u> your right arm, and then <u>step</u> forward on your left foot. As you step, <u>bring</u> the ball back behind you.

Do you know the part of speech of the underlined words? They're verbs, or words of action. Each verb tells the action that must be taken during a step in the process.

When you explain how to do something, it's important to include all the steps in the process. If you give incomplete instructions, your readers won't be able to reach their goal.

Also, be sure to explain specialized words and tools. Remember that your readers' background and experience may be different from your own. For example, if you do a lot of cooking, you probably know the specialized term *sauté*. Because you know the word, you may believe that everyone else does too. However, people who don't cook may need to have the word explained. They may have heard the word without knowing exactly what it means.

When you write a how-to essay, put yourself in your readers' place. Think of ways to help your readers understand the process you're explaining.

In Your Journal

Can you cut someone's hair? Explain the best route from one place to another? Do a magic trick? Sink a basketball? Start a list of things you know how to do. It will come in handy when you write a how-to essay.

Exercise 2

PART A
Underline the action word or words in each step.

To make a California sandwich, take two pieces of wheat bread. Spread one piece of bread with a teaspoon of mayonnaise. Then, put a slice of Colby cheese on top of the mayonnaise. Layer lettuce, bean sprouts, and tomato on top of the cheese. Cover the sandwich with the second piece of bread and cut the sandwich in half.

PART B
Suppose you have to explain to a child how to use a push-button telephone. What steps should the child take? List them. Underline the verb or verbs in each step.

_____

_____

_____

_____

PART C
Which of the following phrases do you know? Choose one and define it. Or define a phrase that describes a process from a hobby or field that you know well.

▶ Basting the hem
▶ Bleeding the brakes
▶ Snapping the football
▶ Choking the guitar string
▶ Creaming the butter and sugar

Definition: _____

_____

Check your answers on page 214.

Organizing Ideas: Time Order

What's the best way to organize a how-to essay? Steps in a how-to essay should be organized in time order. Otherwise, readers will end up very confused. Imagine trying to follow disorganized instructions like these:

> Put six chicken thighs in a well-greased baking dish. Cover and bake at 350° for fifty minutes. Before you put the dish in the oven, put a bed of rice underneath the chicken. You should marinate (soak) the chicken for several hours in a good teriyaki sauce. I like Johnson's, which you can find at almost any grocery store. Be sure to preheat the oven. The rice tastes better if you put a few cooked mushrooms and a little melted butter in it.

The recipe is difficult to follow because the steps aren't in the right order. Here are the revised instructions:

> Marinate (soak) six chicken thighs in teriyaki sauce for several hours. My favorite sauce is Johnson's, which you can buy at almost any grocery store.
>
> About an hour and a half before serving time, cook enough white rice to make three cups. Follow the instructions on the box. While the rice is cooking, melt three tablespoons of butter over low heat. Add a half cup of sliced mushrooms and cook until tender. When the rice is ready, stir in the mushrooms and butter.
>
> Next, put the rice mixture in the bottom of a well-greased baking dish. Spread it around evenly so that it forms a bed. Then, put the marinated thighs on the rice.
>
> Finally, cover the chicken and bake it at 350° for fifty minutes or until done.

The new instructions are easier to follow because the steps are more clearly organized (and fully explained). Notice also that the steps in the new instructions are introduced by **transitions**. Words such as *then, while,* and *next* link one step to the next. The transitions help readers keep track of what must be done and when to do a step. Be sure to use time-order transitions to link the steps in your how-to essays.

Time-Order Transitions

first	now	when	while
second	then	after	next
third	meanwhile	before	finally

Exercise 3

Put the steps below in time order. Number the first step 1, the second step 2, and so on. Then use the steps to write a paragraph. Be sure to link the steps with time-order transitions.

Topic: Going grocery shopping

_____ Get a shopping cart.

_____ Make a grocery list.

_____ Go to the store.

_____ Pay the cashier.

_____ Empty your cart at the checkout.

_____ Go up and down the aisles, selecting food.

_____ Take your food home.

Paragraph: _____

_____

_____

_____

_____

_____

Check your answers on page 215.

Read How-To Essays

You've studied three elements of how-to essays: the main idea, or goal to be reached; the steps involved in reaching the goal; and the order in which to put the steps. Look for these elements as you read the following essays.

Do you cook or bake? Alexander G. McCurdy's recipe will give you a new approach to an old standard—chicken. Jessica B. Harris's recipe will help you make the perfect pie crust.

Chicken Parmesan McCurdy

by Alexander G. McCurdy

(1) Although all single parents have less time to prepare meals, single dads are the most likely to be expected to survive only on instant microwave meals. Various circumstances (economy not the least) caused me to become a little more adept in the kitchen. My recipe for Chicken Parmesan McCurdy is fairly easy. You will need:

1 boneless chicken breast (per person)
1 package of Shake'n Bake (original flavor)
1 cup egg noodles, cooked (per person)
2 ounces picante sauce, hot or mild to your taste (per person)
1 ounce grated cheese (per person)

(2) Preheat the oven to 350°. Trim fat and skin from the chicken, and soak the breasts in picante sauce. Do not rinse. Shake each piece individually in the Shake'n Bake bag. Place chicken on cooking tray and bake for 20–25 minutes (or until done). While the chicken is baking, boil the noodles according to package directions, and drain as soon as done.

(3) While the noodles are boiling and the chicken baking, put the picante sauce into microwave-safe cups and "nuke" for about 2 minutes (until hot). Just about now, the chicken should be done, so place the noodles on the plate, lay a piece of chicken on top, pour the sauce over, and sprinkle with grated cheese. Now serve to the waiting horde (children).

(4) I get the kids to make some garlic bread while I pour myself a little red wine; then we all sit down to enjoy a great meal.

Pie Crust

by Jessica B. Harris

(1) OK. It's confession time. I do not make wonderful pie crust. My mother does, however. For years now I've been badgering her for the recipe. Her usual response is "It's simple. The trick is to handle the dough as little as possible. Handling it makes it tough." Finally, I managed to get her to write it down, and I followed her through the steps. Here it is.

½ teaspoon salt

Yield = one 9-inch pie crust

1 cup sifted all-purpose flour

⅓ cup lard (if substituting vegetable shortening, use an additional 2 tablespoons)

3 tablespoons ice water

(2) Add the salt to the flour, then cut the lard into the mixture with a pastry blender or two knives or the tips of your fingers (THE IDEA IS TO HANDLE THE PASTRY AS LITTLE AS POSSIBLE) until it has the texture of cornmeal. Then gradually add the water, a few drops at a time, continuing to mix lightly. When all of the flour mixture is moistened, form it into a thick, flat disk. Wrap the dough in wax paper and chill it in the refrigerator for 30 minutes.

(3) Remove the dough and place it on a floured surface. Using a rolling pin, roll the dough away from the center using light, even strokes and rolling in only one direction until there is a circle of dough large enough to fit into the pie plate. Place the dough in the pie plate and pinch the edges between your thumb and forefinger to flute the edges. Prick the bottom of the pie crust with a fork to release the air while it is cooking. Place the crust in a preheated 450-degree oven and bake for 15 to 18 minutes or until golden brown. Remove from the oven and cool. It is now ready to use for any mixture requiring a precooked pie crust. For a mixure that requires a partially cooked pie crust, reduce the cooking to 10 minutes.

Check Your Understanding

....

Answer each question about "Chicken Parmesan McCurdy" and "Pie Crust." Look back at the essays if you need to.

1. What is the main idea of "Chicken Parmesan McCurdy"? Circle the letter.

   (a) Single fathers should learn how to cook.

   (b) Follow the instructions to make a chicken dish.

2. According to the author, what are the benefits of making his chicken dish? Circle the letter.

   (a) It's quick and easy.

   (b) It's low in fat and calories.

3. What order should the following steps be in? Number the first step 1, the second step 2, and so on.

   _____ Heat the picante sauce in the microwave oven.
   _____ Bake the chicken until done.
   _____ Preheat the oven to 350°.
   _____ Layer the noodles, chicken, sauce, and cheese.
   _____ Coat each piece of chicken with Shake'n Bake.
   _____ Trim the fat and skin from the chicken.
   _____ Boil and drain the noodles.

4. What is the main idea of "Pie Crust"? Circle the letter.

   (a) Follow the steps to make a wonderful pie crust.

   (b) Harris's mother makes a wonderful pie crust.

5. What does the term *flute* (paragraph 3) mean? Circle the letter.

   (a) To roll out dough using light, even strokes

   (b) To pinch crust edges between the forefinger and thumb

6. What time order transitions does Harris use in her essay? List three.

   (a)

   (b)

   (c)

Check your answers on page 215.

■ Write a How-To Essay

Prewriting: Selecting a Topic and Purpose

Alexander G. McCurdy and Jessica B. Harris give step-by-step instructions in their recipes. **Write a how-to essay in which you give step-by-step instructions.** Your purpose is to explain. The topic you choose could be

▶ A life skill

▶ A sport or athletic skill

▶ A job skill

▶ A skill used in a hobby

Below are some ideas to help you get started. Choose *one* of these topics or use one of your own. You may also want to check your journal. See if you have written about something you do well that you would enjoy explaining to someone else in an essay.

▶ How to start a car

▶ How to paint a wall

▶ How to cook a certain dish

▶ How to shoot a basket

▶ How to lift weights

▶ How to cut a child's hair

▶ How to give a baby a bath

▶ How to diaper a baby

▶ How to put on makeup

Write your topic below.

Topic: _____

Prewriting: Developing Your Topic

Now that you have your topic, you need to develop it. Think of the steps in the process you're going to explain. Picture the process in your mind. Imagine yourself going slowly through it. As you imagine, freewrite. (You learned about freewriting in Chapter 2.) To freewrite, put your pencil or pen on the paper and keep writing. As you imagine the process, write down everything you see in your mind.

Here's one student's freewriting about how to do a sit-up.

I'm lying on my back with my hands clasped behind my head and my knees bent. My feet are on the floor. My elbows are bent and are resting on the floor too. Slowly, I pull my tummy muscles in while I push down my lower back. My shoulders and head raise off the ground. I'm breathing out at this point. I hold myself up for a little bit and then come back down, breathing out. Oh, yeah—all this time my head is tilted back and my eyes are looking toward the ceiling.

Now, picture yourself doing the skill you want to explain. On the lines below, freewrite about all the steps you see yourself going through.

_____

_____

_____

_____

_____

_____

_____

_____

_____

Prewriting: Organizing Your Ideas

Finish prewriting by organizing your ideas.

▶ **Write a main idea sentence.**

Ask yourself, What goal do I want my readers to reach?

Main idea sentence: _____

_____

▶ **Now, group the steps in your process.**

Decide if you need one, two, or more paragraphs for the body of your essay. Draw a line around the steps that go together. Or, if you prefer, draw clusters showing how the steps go together.

▶ **Decide what order to put your steps in.**

Number your steps in the order you want them in. Follow the student example.

I'm lying on my back with my hands clasped behind my head and my knees bent. My feet are on the floor. My elbows are bent and are resting on the floor too. Slowly, I pull my tummy muscles in while I push down my lower back. My shoulders and head raise of the ground. I'm breathing out at this point. I hold myself up for a little bit and then come back down, breathing out. Oh, yeah—all this time my head is tilted back and my eyes are looking toward the ceiling.

Drafting

The next stage of the writing process is drafting. During this stage, you use your prewriting plan to write. Remember that a first draft is just a first try. You'll have a chance to improve your writing when you revise and edit.

Using your plan, write a first draft on the topic of your choice. If you need more space, write on another piece of paper.

STATE A
GOAL IN THE
INTRODUCTION.

_____

_____

_____

_____

_____

INTRODUCE
STEPS WITH
TRANSITIONS.

_____

_____

_____

_____

_____

_____

_____

_____

_____

END WITH A
RESTATEMENT
OF THE GOAL.

_____

_____

Revising

The next stage is to evaluate your draft, alone or with a partner. First, do the Revision Warm-Up. Then use the Revision Checklist to revise your draft.

Revision Warm-Up

Follow the directions below.

1. Find a step that's out of order. Draw an arrow to show where it belongs.
2. Add these two steps where they best belong:

▶ As you rise, breathe out.
▶ As you lower, breathe in.

Sit Up!

These days, exercise is important. So is avoiding injury. Sit-ups can keep you fit, but you must be careful to do them properly.

It's important to start out in the correct position. Keep your feet on the floor, about shoulder distance apart. Lie on your back with your knees up and bent. Clasp your hands and rest them on the back of your neck.

Now, pull in your lower "tummy" muscles. At the same time, push your lower back into the floor. Your head and shoulders should naturally rise from the floor. Be sure to keep your head and elbows back and look toward the ceiling. Hold this position; then relax and lower your upper body.

Follow these steps, and you'll do sit-ups correctly. Soon, you'll have a firmer and more attractive tummy.

Check your answers on page 215.

🖎 **Revision Checklist**

Yes	No	
☐	☐	**1.** Does the introductory paragraph state a goal?
☐	☐	**2.** Does the introduction include a benefit of learning the process?
☐	☐	**3.** Does the body include all the steps in the process?
☐	☐	**4.** Are the steps in time order?
☐	☐	**5.** Are the steps linked by time-order transitions?
☐	☐	**6.** Does the essay have a concluding paragraph?
☐	☐	**7.** Are all the steps in the process clear?

Editing

The last stage of the writing process is editing. During this stage, you look for and correct errors in grammar, mechanics, and usage.

Do the Editing Exercise. Then look for and correct any noun, pronoun, and verb errors as well as any other errors in your draft. If possible, work with a partner.

Editing Exercise: Verbs

Underline and correct the verb error in each sentence.

Two Different People

My ex-girlfriend and I seen eye to eye on very few things. One of the many things we couldn't agreed on was movies.

She liked action pictures—the kind in which the bad guys are kill off by a hero. She wasn't happy unless a car or two and maybe a building were blew up during the course of the story. I have always hate violent pictures. I like upbeat, well-wrote stories about people overcoming their problems.

One Saturday night, our differences come to a head. We have just finished dinner and were arguing about what movie to see. She has been wanting to see an Arnold Schwarzenegger movie, whereas I wanted to see a movie about baseball. As we argued, each of us grown more stubborn.

Finally, we done the only thing we could do. We gone to the same theater but not to the same movie. That very evening, we breaked off our relationship. We haven't spoke to each other since. I should have knew better than to date someone whose taste was so different from mine.

Check your answers on page 215.

CHAPTER 6 | GIVING EXAMPLES

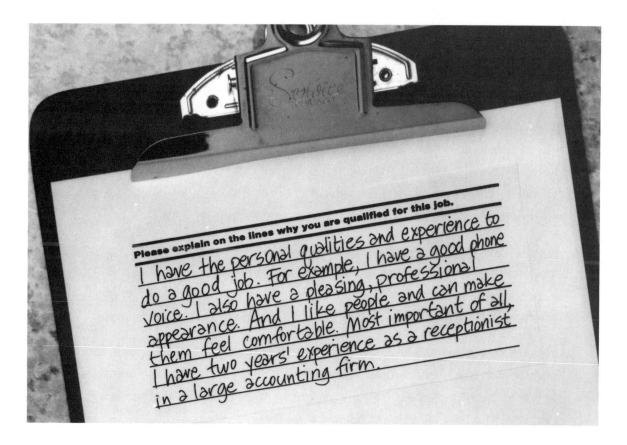

Is the person who wrote the paragraph above qualified for the job? She says she is. Then she goes on to explain why by giving examples. Since the examples are well chosen, you're likely to agree with the applicant. She does seem qualified for the job. Giving examples is a common way of explaining. In this chapter, you'll learn how to use examples to explain and support a main idea.

AFTER WORKING THROUGH THIS CHAPTER, YOU SHOULD BE ABLE TO

▶ FIND THE MAIN IDEA OF AN ESSAY THAT GIVES EXAMPLES

▶ IDENTIFY SUPPORTING EXAMPLES

▶ ORGANIZE EXAMPLES IN ORDER OF IMPORTANCE

▶ PREWRITE, DRAFT, REVISE, AND EDIT AN ESSAY OF EXAMPLE

■ Elements of Essays of Example

This section answers three basic questions about the essay of example: What is its structure? Why use examples? What are some ways to organize the essay?

Main Idea: General Statement

An essay of example often starts out with a general comment, or statement. The statement could be about the world. It could be about life or people. Or it could be about the writer himself or herself. The general statement is the essay's main idea.

The essay then goes on to give examples that support the statement. The whole point of the essay is to show why the general statement is true. The essay below follows this statement-and-example pattern.

Who Cares?

I'd heard before I moved here that this was an unfriendly town. It was said that the people who live here just don't care about each other. In the short time I've lived here, I've learned different. People here are always willing to help out.

Often, when someone is facing huge medical expenses, neighbors raise money to pay for the bills. For example, last weekend my church group ran a special car wash. We collected $500 for the Wilkinses, to help pay for their child's operation. The Elks club also is holding a fund-raising dinner.

Another example of people's caring attitude is the town's new shelter for the homeless. Most of the day-to-day work of running the shelter is done by volunteers. They greet people at the door and answer the phones. They discuss job leads with clients and serve them hot coffee. They also hand out blankets and bedrolls and do a thousand other chores.

The literacy program at our public library is yet another example of people's caring attitude. Many townspeople support the program by acting as volunteer tutors. They give up their free time to help other adults learn to read and write. Volunteers also run an after-school tutoring program. There, children can go for help with their homework.

These are just a few of the townspeople's acts of kindness. Though I haven't been here long, I've seen many more. I'm proud to say that the people in this town truly care about each other.

The main idea is that the townspeople are always willing to help each other. Each paragraph in the body gives an example or examples to support this general statement.

Exercise 1

Read the essay. Then underline the main idea in the introduction.

Too Much Violence

Our kids see too much violence on TV. I realized this about my own children just last Saturday.

That morning, my three kids watched cartoons. Every time I glanced at the TV, a cartoon character was kicking or hitting or shooting another character.

That afternoon, the kids watched an old Three Stooges movie. The children giggled when Moe pulled out Larry's hair. The kids howled with laughter when Moe poked Curly in the eye. I was not amused—especially when the kids began imitating what they saw.

Unfortunately, the worst violence the kids saw was on the TV news that night. Story after story told about a real person being hurt or killed by someone else. Is it really necessary to report on every violent crime?

Viewing all that violence has got to have a bad effect on children. These days, kids grow up too fast as it is. Parents don't need TV speeding up the process.

Check your answers on page 215.

IN YOUR JOURNAL

Your journal is an excellent place to comment on things. You can observe the world and write about what you see. When you make a comment, also note one or two examples that made you make the comment. Here are some general statements to help you get started. Choose one or two. Add examples to support the comment.

- ▶ TV is filled with annoying commercials.
- ▶ This year's fashions are crazier than ever.
- ▶ There are a lot of bad drivers on the road these days.
- ▶ Hard times can bring out the best in people.

Developing the Main Idea: Examples

You've seen how examples can be used to support a general statement. But what, exactly, *is* an example? An **example** is a specific instance or case. A general statement, or main idea, is "big." It might refer to many people, places, or things. In contrast, an example is "small." It refers to fewer people, places, or things. Look again at the essay on page 80. Think about the relationship between the general statement ("People here are always willing to help out") and the examples that support it.

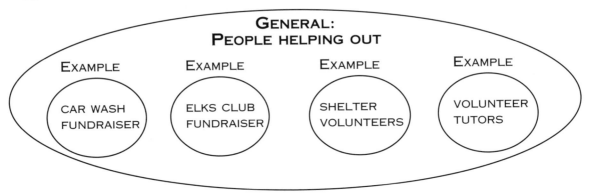

The bigger circle stands for the general statement. This circle includes everyone in the community. The smaller circles stand for the examples. Each refers to a smaller group of people within the community.

Examples are used in all kinds of writing. But they are especially important to writing that explains. That's because examples show what a writer means.

Imagine reading an essay and finding this general statement: "You should devote yourself to the things that really matter." To you, "the things that really matter" might be earning money and building a career. To another reader, "the things that really matter" might refer to home and family. Other readers may have still other meanings for the general words. Did the writer mean all of these ideas—or none? Examples would clear up the mystery.

When you make a general statement, don't make your readers wonder what you mean. Back up the "big" with the "little," and explain by giving examples.

WITH A PARTNER

Together, choose one or two of the general ideas below. Write down examples that show what the idea or ideas mean to you. Do not talk over or show each other your examples. When you're both finished, compare notes. Did the idea or ideas mean exactly the same thing to both of you?

▶ A good job ▶ A great time

▶ A delicious meal ▶ The best music

Exercise 2

Following are main ideas for three different essays. From the list of examples, choose examples that explain each general statement. Write the examples on the lines below each statement.

Examples

▶ There's the deep and vast Grand Canyon.

▶ Salsa now outsells ketchup.

▶ Store clerks are impatient when they can't understand you.

▶ You can't understand what people are saying on TV shows.

▶ There's the high, snowcapped Rocky Mountains.

▶ There's the huge, watery Everglades swamp.

▶ There are more than 50 Mexican restaurants in the city.

▶ You can't ask for directions.

▶ Tortilla chips and salsa seem to be served at every party.

General Statements

1. Mexican food is becoming more and more popular.

_____

_____

_____

2. There's a national park for you, no matter what kind of landscape you like.

_____

_____

_____

3. Living in a country where you don't speak the language is difficult.

_____

_____

_____

Check your answers on page 216.

Organizing Ideas: Order of Importance

Sometimes, all the examples in an essay are equally important. Each carries the same weight in supporting the main idea. Look again at the essay "Who Cares?" on page 80. Each example in the essay is just as important as the others.

Main Idea ⟶ The townspeople are willing to help each other.

Example 1 ⟶ One important example: church fundraiser

Example 2 ⟶ One important example: Elks fundraiser

Example 3 ⟶ One important example: shelter volunteers

Example 4 ⟶ One important example: volunteer tutors

In other essays, one or two examples may be more important than the others. To show which examples carry the most weight, writers may put them in **order of importance**—from least to most important. Look again at the job application at the beginning of the chapter. It is organized in order of importance.

Main Idea ⟶ I have the qualities and experience to do a good job.

Example 1 ⟶ Least important example: good phone voice

Example 2 ⟶ More important example: pleasing appearance

Example 3 ⟶ More important example: like people

Example 4 ⟶ Most important example: two years' experience

Concluding with the best example helped the writer build a strong case. She ended on her strongest, rather than weakest, note.

Notice the transition that the writer used to link the last example. She began the sentence with the words *most important of all*. There are other transitions that show order of importance. For example, say you're giving examples of good times in your life. The transition for the last example could be "The *best* time in my life was . . ." If you're giving examples of bad times, you'd write, "The *worst* time in my life was . . ."

When you place examples in order of importance, use a transition that shows the most important, dramatic, or extreme example is coming last.

Order-of-Importance Transitions

little—less—least

much—more—most

good—better—best

bad—worse—worst

Exercise 3

Read the essay. Then circle the letter of the type of organization used in the essay.

Annoying Co-worker

I like almost everyone I work with. However, there's one co-worker who really annoys me. His name is Barry, and he has some very bad habits.

One bad habit is that he borrows items without asking. Whenever I'm not around, he takes my pen or my glue or my scissors. Then, when I reach for my supplies, they're not there.

Worse yet, Barry makes a lot of personal phone calls. And he doesn't lower his voice when he's on the phone. I try to focus on my work. But it's hard when Barry is yak-yak-yakking with his girlfriend.

Perhaps Barry's worst habit is butting into other people's conversations. On three different occasions, he has interrupted me while I was talking with a client. Each time, I was answering a question. Each time, Barry said I was answering the question wrong. (I wasn't.) It was very embarrassing.

I've talked to Barry about his annoying habits. Every time, he said he was sorry and would change. But he hasn't, and I doubt that he ever will.

(a) equal importance

(b) order of importance

Check your answers on page 216.

Read an Essay of Example

You've studied three elements of an essay that gives examples: the general-statement main idea, examples, and ways to organize examples. Look for these elements as you read the following essay.

On radio and TV, Charles Osgood comments about the world around him. He also writes a column that appears in many newspapers. You may have heard or read his commentaries. Like many of us, Osgood thinks the world does not always change for the better. In the following essay, he gives examples to show why he thinks so.

Improvements

by Charles Osgood

(1) I recently saw an ad for a commuter airline about a new, "improved" baggage service. The improvement is that instead of the airline carrying your bags out to the plane, you get to carry the bags out to the plane yourself. This is typical of what passes for improvements these days.

(2) When they say any service has been "improved," what they usually mean now is that they've figured a way for you to do it so that they don't have to do it.

(3) In a bank, you used to hand your checks and deposit or withdrawal slips to one of the tellers, and he or she would put the slips in different places and push different buttons and then hand you the cash or deposit receipt. Now they have improved banking service so much that nobody does anything for you. Instead of waiting on line for a teller, you wait on line for a machine. Then you push all the buttons yourself. Then if there's any mistake, you have only yourself to blame. This may not be better for you, but it's better for the bank.

(4) It started with the supermarkets. I can remember when you'd go to the grocery store and tell the grocer what you wanted and he'd find it, take it down from the shelves, and put it in a paper bag for you. Now things have improved a lot. You find it. You lift it into the shopping cart and later onto the checkout counter. About half the time you bag it yourself, and carry it out to the car yourself. I don't mind doing all this, you understand, but I fail to see in what way it is better.

(5) To make a long-distance phone call, all you used to have to do was tell the operator what city and phone number you wanted. She'd get it for you. Sometimes you'd hear her talking operator-talk to some other

operator, with codes and all that. Now you are your own operator and do all the work yourself. This may not seem like such a good idea to you, but it seems like a wonderful idea to the phone companies.

(6) There used to be an elevator man in our building. His name was Bill. Bill knew what floor I got off on. I never had to tell him. He ran the elevator, opened and closed the door, and we would exchange a word or two about the weather. Several years ago, Bill was replaced by a panel of buttons. The doors open and close by themselves. Sometimes they close while somebody is standing right in the doorway. The doors don't care. They are the new, improved doors that go with the new, improved elevator.

(7) The fellow at the gas station used to pump the gas into your car. He would also volunteer to check your oil and would always wipe your windshield. Now, under the new, improved kind of filling station, unless you want to pay more for it, you pump the gas. You check the oil. If you're lucky, they'll lend you a rag to wipe the dipstick. And if you expect to see through the windshield, you had better wipe it yourself. They will lend you another rag. Or more likely the same rag.

(8) I am not sure we can stand very many more of these improvements. It is clear now that when companies tell you they're doing things *better* now, they don't mean better for you. They mean better for them.

Check Your Understanding

PART A

Answer each question about "Improvements." Look back at the essay if you need to.

1. What is the main idea of "Improvements"? Circle the letter.

   (a) Most things today are better than they were in the past.

   (b) So-called "improvements" in services benefit businesses, not customers.

2. What six examples did Osgood use to support his main idea? List them. Then tell in which paragraph each example appears. The first example has been listed for you.

   (a) _"Improved" baggage service – first paragraph_

   (b) _____

   (c) _____

   (d) _____

   (e) _____

   (f) _____

3. Which order did Osgood put the examples in? Circle the letter.

   (a) equal importance

   (b) order of importance

PART B

Answer each question in a sentence or two.

1. What other examples could Osgood have used to explain his main idea? Write an example based on your own experiences.

   _____

   _____

2. Where in the conclusion does Osgood restate the main idea? Copy it.

   _____

Check your answers on page 216.

■ Write an Essay of Example

Prewriting: Selecting a Topic and Purpose

In "Improvements," Charles Osgood makes a general statement about the world today. Then, he lists examples to show what he means. **Write your own essay about something happening in the world today.**

Look around you, and make a comment about people or events you see. Include examples to show what you mean. Your purpose is to explain. The topic you choose could be

- ▶ Everyday living
- ▶ Sports
- ▶ Fashion
- ▶ Politics

Below are some ideas to help you get started. Choose *one* of these topics or use one of your own. You may also want to check your journal. See if you have made a general comment that you would enjoy explaining in an essay. Don't forget to use descriptive details to help your readers picture your examples.

- ▶ Ways in which everyday life is easier than in the past
- ▶ People acting rude these days
- ▶ Different ways you enjoy spending your free time
- ▶ Some great athletes who are playing today
- ▶ Clothes that have come back into style
- ▶ Some ways the government works (or doesn't work) for us

Write your topic below.

Topic:_____

Prewriting: Developing Your Topic

Now that you have your topic, you need to think of examples to develop it. Brainstorming is a good way to get ideas for an essay of example. (You learned about brainstorming in Chapter 2.)

Here are a student's brainstormed notes. His topic was bad drivers.

1. Don't see stop signs

2. So busy combing hair don't notice light has changed

3. Forget to use turn signals

4. Speed on side streets

5. Don't care if kids get hurt

6. Tailgate all the time

On the lines below, list examples to develop your topic. Follow the student example and use brainstorming. Or, if you prefer, use a different method, such as questioning or freewriting.

_____

_____

_____

_____

_____

_____

_____

_____

_____

_____

Prewriting: Organizing Your Ideas

Finish prewriting by organizing your ideas.

▶ **Write a main idea sentence.**

Your main idea is the general statement, or comment, you want to make. If you're not sure what your general statement is, ask yourself, What are most of my examples about?

Main idea sentence: _____

_____

▶ **Now, group your supporting examples.**

Decide if you need one, two, or more paragraphs for the body of your essay. Draw a line around the examples that go together in each paragraph. Or, if you prefer, draw clusters showing how the examples go together. Follow the student example.

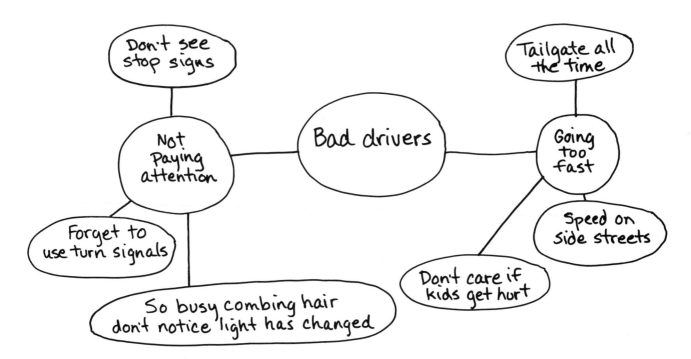

▶ **Decide what order to put your supporting examples in.**

Are some of your examples more important than others? Or are all your examples of equal importance? Decide which order to put your examples in. **Write the order below.**

Order: _____

If you want, number your examples to show the order you want them in.

Drafting

The next stage of the writing process is drafting. During this stage, you use your prewriting plan to write. Remember that a first draft is just a first try. You'll have a chance to improve your writing when you revise and edit.

Using your plan, write a first draft on the topic of your choice. If you need more space, write on another piece of paper.

INCLUDE A GENERAL STATEMENT MAIN IDEA IN THE INTRODUCTION.

_____

_____

_____

_____

_____

_____

USE SPECIFIC EXAMPLES TO DEVELOP THE MAIN IDEA.

_____

_____

_____

_____

_____

_____

_____

END WITH A RESTATEMENT OF THE MAIN IDEA.

_____

Revising

The next stage is to evaluate your first draft, alone or with a partner. First, do the Revision Warm-Up. Then use the Revision Checklist to revise your draft.

Revision Warm-Up

Follow the directions below.

1. Add a transition to the beginning of paragraph 3 to show that the most important examples are coming up.
2. Add a concluding paragraph that includes a restatement of the main idea.

Bad Drivers

Every time I drive, I can't help noticing. Drivers are getting worse and worse. I'm surprised that the accident rate isn't higher than it is.

Too many people just don't pay attention to their driving. When they go to make a turn, they forget to use their turn signals. They're so busy changing the station on the radio or combing their hair that they don't seem to notice the light has changed. They also run stop signs.

Many people also drive much too fast. I see tailgaters every time I drive on the highway. They're in such a hurry that they don't keep a safe distance from the other drivers. Speeding drivers have also made the side streets dangerous. The street I live on used to be quiet, but speeding cars have made it unsafe. The speeders just don't care about the kids playing near the street. Will it take a tragedy to make these drivers slow down?

Check your answers on page 216.

☑ Revision Checklist

Yes	No	
☐	☐	**1.** Is there a main idea sentence or sentences in the introduction?
☐	☐	**2.** Is the body well developed with examples?
☐	☐	**3.** Do all the examples explain, or support, the main idea?
☐	☐	**4.** Are the examples logically organized?
☐	☐	**5.** Does the conclusion help sum up the main idea?
☐	☐	**6.** Are all the sentences and ideas clear?

Editing

The last stage of the writing process is editing. During this stage, you look for and correct errors in grammar, mechanics, and usage.

Do the Editing Exercise. Then look for and correct any noun, pronoun, verb, and adjective and adverb errors in your draft. Also look for other kinds of errors. If possible, work with a partner.

Editing Exercise: Adjectives and Adverbs

Underline and correct the adjective or adverb error in each sentence.

Picky Pet

My cat, Murphy, is the most pickiest eater in the world. I've given her every brand of cat food on the market, and she doesn't like none of them. Each time that I give her a new brand, she acts as if it's the worse food she's ever eaten. Yesterday, I finally decided to do something to make her less fussier. I decided I wouldn't give her nothing to eat until she'd cleaned her plate.

Last night, she began to meow pitiful. She hadn't touched the food I'd given her, and it looked terribly. It had been sitting so long that it was complete dry. She continued to meow sad, but I pretended to ignore her.

Suddenly, I heard a loudly noise in the kitchen. I quick ran to see what had happened. Murphy had flipped her bowl over and was making the worstest mess I'd ever seen. The cat meowed loud and happily as I opened a can of tuna. I hated to give in, but I figured it was more better than putting up with her tantrums.

Check your answers on page 216.

CHAPTER 7 | COMPARING AND CONTRASTING

Which of the two candidates would you vote for? To decide, you might compare and contrast each candidate's views with your own. From voting to shopping, comparing and contrasting are useful thinking skills. In this chapter, you'll learn how to write essays that compare and contrast.

AFTER WORKING THROUGH THIS CHAPTER, YOU SHOULD BE ABLE TO
- ▶ IDENTIFY TWO REASONS FOR COMPARING AND CONTRASTING
- ▶ SHOW COMPARISON IN CHART FORM
- ▶ ORGANIZE A COMPARISON AND CONTRAST ESSAY
- ▶ PREWRITE, DRAFT, REVISE, AND EDIT AN ESSAY THAT COMPARES AND CONTRASTS

■ Elements of Comparison and Contrast Essays

This section looks at the why, the what, and the how of comparison and contrast essays. You'll see why writers compare and contrast, what bases of comparison they use, and how they organize comparison and contrast essays.

Main Idea: Why Compare and Contrast?

Writers compare and contrast to make a point. Many times, the point is to show that one person or thing is better than another. Read the comparison and contrast essay below. The writer's point, or main idea, is to explain why Stephen Marks would make a better representative than Stella Cisneros.

Mark Your Ballot for Marks

You should look closely at the views of Stephen Marks and Stella Cisneros. If you study their stands on the issues, you'll vote for Marks.

Both Marks and Cisneros have promised to support a two-week waiting period on gun purchases. While the candidates agree on gun control, that is where their similarities end.

Marks wants to hold the line on taxes. In fact, if elected, he would support a two-year tax freeze. In contrast, Cisneros would raise our taxes. She simply doesn't appreciate how hard we taxpayers work for our money.

Marks and Cisneros differ on another important issue—abortion. Marks supports family values. He is against abortion except in cases of rape or incest. Cisneros, on the other hand, wants all women to have unlimited access to abortion.

A final difference between the candidates is their stands on the proposed downtown casino gambling complex. Marks supports it because it will bring jobs and tax dollars. Predictably, Cisneros is against the complex.

The choice is clear. Vote for low taxes, family values, and jobs. Mark your ballot for Marks.

Writers also may compare and contrast simply to show similarities and differences. For example, a writer might compare and contrast her twin brothers to make the point that their personalities differ. Or she might compare and contrast a favorite place during summer and winter to show how it changes over time.

Exercise 1

Read each essay. Then circle the letter of the main idea.

East and West

1. Both New York and Los Angeles are large U.S. cities. Yet the two cities couldn't possibly be more different.

   New York is a tall, dense city. Its skyscrapers rise to the clouds. Its people are squeezed onto islands and along two rivers. They always seem to be in a hurry and are never very friendly.

   On the other hand, Los Angeles is a low, vast city. It stretches over miles. Its people live in valleys and canyons, on foothills and mountains. They are, in general, friendly and relaxed.

   (a) New York is a better place to live than Los Angeles.

   (b) New York and Los Angeles are quite different.

Railway or Highway?

2. Air fares are going up. As a result, travelers are turning to cheaper modes of travel. The old reliables—the bus and the train—are back in demand. Of the two, the bus is the better bargain.

   Both the train and the bus can be relaxing. Both offer scenic views of the countryside. Both serve most major cities. And both generally cost much less than flying. But bus fare is usually less than train fare. I compared train and bus fares from Chicago to three cities—New York, Dallas, and Los Angeles. In each case, bus fare was at least 10 percent less.

   In general, the train is faster and more comfortable. But if cost really matters to you, you'd better go by bus.

   (a) Bus travel is a better bargain than train travel.

   (b) Buses and trains have their good points and bad points.

   Check your answers on page 217.

Developing the Main Idea: Bases of Comparison

How do writers make comparisons and contrasts? They look for similarities and differences in the people or things they're writing about. The qualities they compare and contrast are called **bases of comparison**.

Look again at the chart at the beginning of this chapter. The chart contains four bases of comparison—taxes, gun control, abortion, and casino gambling. Comparing and contrasting the candidates' views on those issues furthered the writer's point—to show that Marks is the better candidate.

When you decide what bases to use, consider your topic and main idea. Like the writer of the political essay, choose bases that help make a point.

For example, suppose that you want to show that one fast-food burger is better than another. What bases of comparison might you choose? You'd probably want to talk about cost, taste, and fat content. These qualities would matter to most diners deciding which burger to buy. A chart would help you keep track of your bases of comparison.

COMPARISON AND CONTRAST CHART

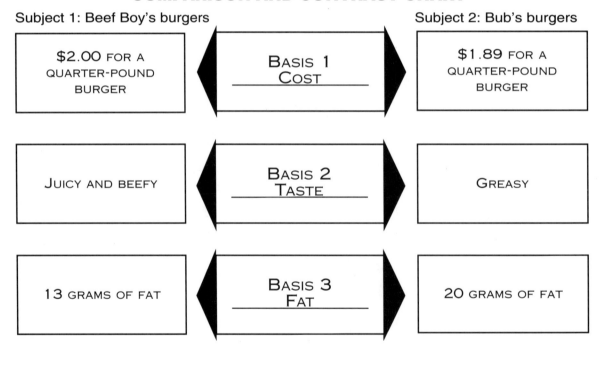

Subject 1: Beef Boy's burgers   Subject 2: Bub's burgers

$2.00 FOR A QUARTER-POUND BURGER	**BASIS 1 COST**	$1.89 FOR A QUARTER-POUND BURGER
JUICY AND BEEFY	**BASIS 2 TASTE**	GREASY
13 GRAMS OF FAT	**BASIS 3 FAT**	20 GRAMS OF FAT

IN YOUR JOURNAL

Compare and contrast two brands of a similar product, such as two brands of shampoo. Decide which qualities to discuss. Chart these bases of comparison.

Exercise 2

Read the essay. Then complete the comparison and contrast chart.

Day and Night

Have you ever heard the saying "Opposites attract"? It describes the relationship between my husband, a morning person, and me, a night person.

Even on weekends, Leon wakes up at 6:00 A.M. He jumps out of bed with a smile, ready to face the day. Meanwhile, I'm curled up in my blanket, tired and grumpy. The only thing that makes me smile is the thought of going back to sleep.

Check in with us in the afternoon, and you'd see the tide turning. After doing chores all morning, Leon's beginning to feel tired. In contrast, I feel completely energized. Guess who's smiling now?

By the evening, my husband's energy level is very low. When we go to the movies, there's only a fifty-fifty chance he'll stay awake till the end of the film. I, on the other hand, wish we could go out afterward.

As you can see, my husband and I are on completely different schedules. He gets up with the roosters, and I fly with the night owls.

COMPARISON AND CONTRAST CHART

Subject 1: Day Person   Subject 2: Night Person

	BASIS 1 ENERGY LEVEL IN MORNING	
	BASIS 2 ENERGY LEVEL IN AFTERNOON	
	BASIS 3 ENERGY LEVEL AT NIGHT	

Check your answers on page 217.

Organizing Ideas: Block and Alternating Patterns

Two good ways to organize comparison and contrast essays are the block and alternating patterns of organization. To use the block pattern, first discuss one subject. Then, in the next block, or paragraph, compare and contrast the second subject with the first.

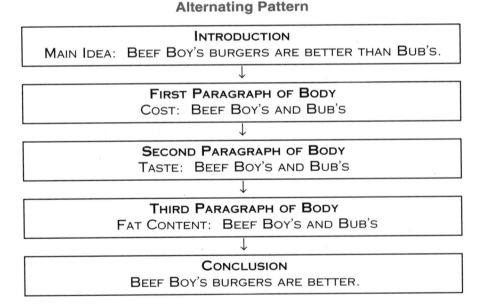

Block Pattern

INTRODUCTION
MAIN IDEA: BEEF BOY'S BURGERS ARE BETTER THAN BUB'S.

↓

FIRST PARAGRAPH OF BODY
COST, TASTE, AND FAT CONTENT OF BUB'S BURGERS

↓

SECOND PARAGRAPH OF BODY
COST, TASTE, AND FAT CONTENT OF BEEF BOY'S BURGERS

↓

CONCLUSION
BEEF BOY'S BURGERS ARE BETTER.

The alternating pattern is different. It is organized around bases of comparison.

Alternating Pattern

INTRODUCTION
MAIN IDEA: BEEF BOY'S BURGERS ARE BETTER THAN BUB'S.

↓

FIRST PARAGRAPH OF BODY
COST: BEEF BOY'S AND BUB'S

↓

SECOND PARAGRAPH OF BODY
TASTE: BEEF BOY'S AND BUB'S

↓

THIRD PARAGRAPH OF BODY
FAT CONTENT: BEEF BOY'S AND BUB'S

↓

CONCLUSION
BEEF BOY'S BURGERS ARE BETTER.

In general, the block pattern works best when you have only a few bases of comparison. When you have several bases, use the alternating method.

When you write a comparison and contrast essay, remember to use appropriate transitions to link your ideas.

Comparison and Contrast Transitions

in comparison	in contrast
in the same way	on the other hand
similar to	however

Exercise 3

Circle the letter of the organizing pattern used in each body.

Body 1

Main idea: It's better to pack a lunch than to buy a carry-out lunch.

First, packing a lunch saves money. A sandwich, salad, and small drink cost me about $6.00 in most take-out places downtown. In contrast, the same lunch costs me only about $3.00 if I make it myself.

I also have more time to relax on my lunch hour when I pack my own lunch. By the time I wait for elevators, traffic lights, and long lines at the restaurant, more than half of my lunch hour has gone by. When I bring my lunch, all I have to do is sit down and enjoy it.

Finally, I control the ingredients in my lunch when I bring it myself. I use low-fat, low-salt meats and cheeses. In addition, I always include fruit and vegetables. My homemade lunches are far more healthful than the average carry-out lunch.

(a) block pattern

(b) alternating pattern

Body 2

Main Idea: The city at night looks very different from the city during the day.

During the day, the view from my window is exciting. Below me is the hustle and bustle of a great city. Honking cars are jammed at the traffic light. Buses packed with people slowly make their way from stop to stop. Men and women scurry across the street on their way to work.

At night, the view from my window is peaceful. All the hustle and bustle of the day is gone. A lone car pulls away from the traffic light, which has just turned green. A bus with only a few passengers hurries by. The sidewalks are empty, except for a couple walking arm in arm.

(a) block pattern

(b) alternating pattern

Check your answers on page 217.

Read a Comparison and Contrast Essay

You've studied three elements of comparison and contrast essays: reasons for making comparisons and contrasts, bases of comparison, and patterns of organization. Look for these elements as you read the following essay.

Have you ever watched the TV show "60 Minutes"? If you have, you've seen Andy Rooney. Rooney comes on at the end of the show and comments on different subjects. Here, he comments on the two major political parties in the United States.

Political Parties

by Andrew A. Rooney

A lot of you probably aren't sure whether you're Republicans or Democrats. We have an election coming up shortly, and you ought to find out what you are. I thought it might help if I explained the difference between Republicans and Democrats.

Democrats believe the trouble started with **Herbert Hoover,**[1] and was worse during the Presidency of **Richard Nixon.**[2]

Republicans believe the trouble started with **Franklin Roosevelt,**[3] and is worse than ever right now.

Democrats leave the dishes in the drying rack on the sink overnight.

Republicans put the dishes away every night.

Republicans play tennis.

---

[1] **Herbert Hoover:** U.S. president (Republican) during the Great Depression

[2] **Richard Nixon:** U.S. president (Republican) who resigned as a result of the Watergate scandal

[3] **Franklin Roosevelt:** U.S. president (Democrat) who started social welfare programs as part of the New Deal

Democrats bowl, unless they're **Kennedy**[4] Democrats, in which case they play tennis too.

Democrats love television, and watch a lot of it.

Republicans hate television. They watch a lot of it too.

Democrats are baseball fans.

Republicans follow college football.

Democrats buy their food on payday once a week at the supermarket.

Republicans go to the grocery store every day.

Democrats usually write with a pencil.

Republicans use pens.

In the summer, Democrats drink beer.

Republicans drink gin and tonic. In the winter, they drink Scotch and soda.

Democrats drink beer.

Republicans think taxes are too high because of the Democrats.

Democrats think taxes are too high because of the Republicans.

Republicans have dinner between seven and eight.

Democrats have supper between five and six.

Democrats drink coffee with cream and sugar, from mugs.

Republicans take theirs black—with cup and saucer.

Democrats don't seal the envelopes of their Christmas cards, which they sign by hand.

Republicans seal the envelopes of their Christmas cards, which have their names printed on them—unless they're very rich Republicans, in which case they sign them by hand. If they're very, very rich, they have someone else sign them.

Democrats believe people are basically good but must be saved from themselves by their government.

Republicans believe people are basically bad but they'll be okay if they're left alone.

A lot of Republicans are more like Democrats used to be, and a lot of Democrats are more like Republicans used to be. If you're still not sure what you are, you're probably a Democrat.

....

------

[4] **John Kennedy:** U.S. president (Democrat) from 1960 to 1963

Check Your Understanding

PART A

Answer each question about "Political Parties." Look back at the essay if you need to.

1. What point is Rooney trying to make by comparing and contrasting? Circle the letter of the correct answer.

   (a) To show that Republicans and Democrats differ

   (b) To show that Republicans are better than Democrats

2. Which of the following bases of comparison did Rooney use to compare and contrast Republicans and Democrats? Circle them.

clothing styles	favorite sports	hairstyles
attitude toward TV	kinds of pets	eating habits
favorite drinks	types of home	blame for taxes
dish-drying habits	food-buying habits	writing tools
favorite cars	dinner times	Christmas cards

3. Which pattern of organization did Rooney use? Circle the letter of the correct answer.

   (a) block method

   (b) alternating method

PART B

Answer each question in a sentence or two.

1. Where in the introduction does Rooney state the main idea? Copy the sentence.

   _____

   _____

2. Do you agree with Rooney's characterizations of Democrats and Republicans? Why or why not?

   _____

   _____

Check your answers on page 217.

Write a Comparison and Contrast Essay

Prewriting: Selecting a Topic and Purpose

In "Political Parties," Andy Rooney compares and contrasts two groups of people. **Write an essay that compares and contrasts two persons, groups of people, places, or things.** Your purpose is to explain. The topic you choose could be

- ► Two people you know well
- ► Men and women
- ► Yourself at two different times in your life
- ► Different ways of accomplishing a goal
- ► A favorite place at different times
- ► Two different brands of the same product

Below are some ideas to help you get started. Choose *one* of these topics or use one of your own. You may also want to check your journal. See if you have written about people, places, or things that you would enjoy comparing and contrasting in an essay.

- ► Two children of yours
- ► Your current boyfriend or girlfriend and your ex
- ► Men's and women's attitudes toward a particular subject
- ► Yourself as you were ten years ago and as you are now
- ► Eating at home and eating in a restaurant
- ► Watching a sporting event on TV and seeing it in person
- ► Sewing an item of clothing and buying it ready-made
- ► Your town's downtown area on a weekday and on Sunday
- ► Your favorite brand of ice cream and another brand

Write your topic below.

Topic: _____

Prewriting: Developing Your Topic

Now that you have your topic, you need to think of bases of comparison to develop it. To decide which qualities to compare and contrast, think about your topic and main idea. Ask yourself, What point do I want to make by comparing and contrasting? Do I want to show that one person, place, or thing is better than another? Or do I simply want to show similarities and differences? The answers to these questions will help you decide which qualities to write about.

Once you've decided which bases of comparison to use, make a comparison and contrast chart. Below is a chart done by a student. Following the example, fill in the blank chart. It's OK if you don't use all the bases of comparison. It's also OK to add more bases if you need to.

COMPARISON AND CONTRAST CHART

Subject 1: _Me at sixteen_

Subject 2: _Me today_

Thought I knew it all	Knowledge of life	Know I have a lot to learn
Had none	Goals	Have clear goals

COMPARISON AND CONTRAST CHART

Subject 1: _____

Subject 2: _____

Prewriting: Organizing Your Ideas

Finish prewriting by organizing your ideas.

▶ **Write a main idea sentence.**

Put your main idea in sentence form.

Main idea sentence:_____

_____

▶ **Now, group your bases of comparison.**

Which pattern of organization will you use—block or alternating? If you have only one or two bases of comparison, the block method will probably work well for you. If you have three or more bases, the alternating pattern may be a better choice.

The student who made the chart decided to use the block method because she had only two bases of comparison. Which pattern of organization will you use? **Write the order below.**

Order:_____

You may also find it helpful to map your essay. If you're using the block method of organization, follow the student example below. If you're using the alternating pattern, look back at page 100 for an example.

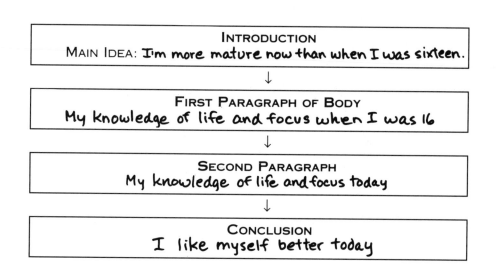

INTRODUCTION
MAIN IDEA: I'm more mature now than when I was sixteen.
↓
FIRST PARAGRAPH OF BODY
My knowledge of life and focus when I was 16
↓
SECOND PARAGRAPH
My knowledge of life and focus today
↓
CONCLUSION
I like myself better today

Drafting

The next stage in the writing process is drafting. During this stage, you use your prewriting plan to write. Remember that a first draft is just a first try. You'll have a chance to improve your writing when you revise and edit.

Using your plan, write a first draft on the topic of your choice. If you need more space, write on another piece of paper.

INCLUDE A CLEAR MAIN IDEA SENTENCE IN THE INTRODUCTION.

_____

_____

_____

_____

_____

_____

_____

USE TRANSITIONS TO INTRODUCE BASES OF COMPARISON.

_____

_____

_____

_____

_____

_____

_____

END BY SUMMING UP THE MAIN IDEA.

_____

_____

Revising

The next stage is to evaluate your draft, alone or with a partner. First, do the Revision Warm-Up. Then use the Revision Checklist to revise your draft.

Revision Warm-Up

Follow the directions below.

1. Write an introduction. Include the main idea sentence the student has already written.

2. Add a conclusion that restates the main idea.

Yesterday and Today

I'm more mature now than when I was sixteen.

When I was sixteen, I was a know-it-all. My parents begged me to stay in school, but I ignored them. They seemed so hopelessly out of touch with the world and my life. Now that I'm twenty-six, I know my parents were right. As a dropout, I haven't been able to get very good jobs. To better myself, I've gone back to school. I know I have a lot to learn.

At sixteen, I had very little focus in life. In fact, I had only two goals. I wanted to get a job so I could buy a nice car and fancy clothes. And I wanted to be friends with the "right" people. In contrast, my goals today are very different. I don't care about fancy clothes or cars. I spend more time with family than with friends. Now, I want to get a good education and find a good job.

Check your answers on page 217.

✍ Revision Checklist

Yes	No	
☐	☐	**1.** Is there a main idea sentence or sentences in the introduction?
☐	☐	**2.** Is the body well developed with bases of comparison?
☐	☐	**3.** Do all the bases of comparison support the main idea?
☐	☐	**4.** Are the bases of comparison logically organized?
☐	☐	**5.** Are ideas linked with transitions?
☐	☐	**6.** Does the conclusion help sum up the main idea?
☐	☐	**7.** Are all the sentences and ideas clear?

Editing

The last stage of the writing process is editing. During this stage, you look for and correct errors in grammar, mechanics, and usage.

Do the Editing Exercise. Then look for and correct any noun, pronoun, verb, adjective and adverb, and sentence structure errors in your draft. Also look for other kinds of errors. If possible, work with a partner.

Editing Exercise: Sentence Structure

Underline and correct the nine errors in sentence structure and punctuation.

On My Own

Should I get my own apartment. That was the question I kept asking myself. Finally, I decided to go ahead and I rented my own place. Though it's expensive being on my own it's well worth it.

I love the freedom of being independent. I answer to no one, I come and go as I please. If I come in at 3 o'clock in the morning. There's no one yelling at me, asking me where I've been.

I also enjoy my new-found privacy. When I lived at home, my little brother was always poking his nose in my business. I couldn't talk on the phone to my friends. Without my little brother listening in on our calls. Now, my life is much better I'm able to keep private things private.

It's expensive to be on my own however I don't mind paying the price. I guess I'm just one of those people. Who are better off being on their own.

Check your answers on page 217.

CHAPTER 8 | PERSUADING

Preserve the park

VALLEY CREEK—Like many of my neighbors, I was shocked to learn that Valley Creek Park may be replaced with a new mini-mall. I will definitely vote against this idea—and others should too. First, Valley Creek Park is the only park within an area of about three square miles. If the park is destroyed, older people and parents with small children will no longer have a recreation area within walking distance. Second, there already are many places to buy groceries, do laundry, and rent videos in this town. We don't need a mini-mall to provide even more! Finally, and most important, the developer of the mini-mall—Right Stuff Property—is owned by Jack O'Connor, the mayor's brother. I think the mall is planned just because O'Connor has "friends in high places" and not because the town needs it. Let's not replace a beautiful park with a bunch of stores no one needs. Vote "no" on the mini-mall referendum.

Elaine S. Su

Above is one kind of persuasive writing—a letter to the editor of a newspaper. Persuasive writing asks readers to think about a subject in a certain way. Often, it also asks readers to take some kind of action.

You use skills in persuasion whenever you try to "sell" your point of view to someone else—be it at home, at school, or on the job. In this chapter, you'll learn more about writing persuasive essays.

AFTER WORKING THROUGH THIS CHAPTER, YOU SHOULD BE ABLE TO

▶ FIND THE OPINION STATED IN A PERSUASIVE ESSAY
▶ DEVELOP REASONS TO SUPPORT AN OPINION
▶ ORGANIZE REASONS EFFECTIVELY
▶ PREWRITE, DRAFT, REVISE, AND EDIT A PERSUASIVE ESSAY

■ Elements of Persuasive Essays

Reread the letter to the editor at the beginning of this chapter. Like all good persuasive writing, it has three key elements. It clearly states an opinion. It gives reasons why readers should share the opinion. And it's organized in a way that builds the best case in support of the opinion.

Main Idea: Stating an Opinion

The main idea sentence of a persuasive essay usually states the writer's **opinion**, or point of view, about a topic. Reread the second sentence of the letter: "I will definitely vote against this idea—and others should too." The writer's point of view (opinion) about the mini-mall (topic) is clear. She's against it. Notice that the main idea also asks readers to take a specific action—vote against the plan.

As you read the following persuasive essay, ask yourself, What's the topic? What opinion does the writer want readers to share? What action does the writer want readers to take?

Do We Need Letter Grades?

Our school district has an interesting plan. It wants to replace letter grades with written evaluations. I think written reports are a great idea.

First, written evaluations would give a clearer picture of a student's abilities. If a student gets an A in algebra, does that mean that the person is equally good at solving all kinds of algebraic problems? Does a student who receives an F know nothing about algebra at all? Written evaluations would give a more complete and accurate evaluation by describing a student's strengths and weaknesses.

In addition, written evaluations would help students study more efficiently. When a student knows what his or her strengths and weaknesses are, he or she also knows what areas to spend the most time on. Students would make better use of study time.

Written reports also would help schools avoid labeling students. Being an F student is embarrassing. All too often, that one letter marks a person as a failure in the eyes of other people. Written reports would treat the student as a whole person, not just a letter grade.

Join me in supporting change in our district's grading system. We all stand to benefit from a switch to written evaluations.

The topic of the essay is grades. The writer's opinion is that written evaluations are better than letter grades. The writer tells readers what action to take at the end of the essay, in the conclusion. If there's a specific action you want your readers to take, you, too, may wait until the end of your persuasive essay to state it.

Exercise 1

Underline the opinion statement in each paragraph.

1. When both husband and wife have full-time jobs, there's no reason why they can't share the household chores. Both are probably tired when they get home. And nothing says only women know how to fix dinner or run the washing machine.

2. Studies show that children find it easier to learn a new language than adults do. In addition, speaking a different language can open up a whole new world for a child. It's never too early for a child to learn to speak a second language.

3. By far, the best way to see the country is by motorcycle. You're not cooped up like you are in a car. You can go places where cars can't go. Finally, you use a lot less gas, so it's easier on your wallet.

Check your answers on page 218.

WITH A PARTNER

Together, read the "Letters to the Editor" page of a local newspaper. Find a letter that states an opinion. Then underline the reasons the writer gives in support of the opinion. Are some of the reasons better than others? Did the writer convince you to share his or her opinion?

IN YOUR JOURNAL

Everyone has opinions. What are some of yours? What do you think about gun control? Heavy metal music? The chances your favorite team will get to the playoffs this year? List several topics of interest to you. For each, write down your opinion about the topic and a few reasons you'd give if you had to sell your opinion to someone else.

Developing the Main Idea: Reasons Why

When you set out to persuade others, you must offer them good reasons why they should share your point of view. You may have a strong opinion about a subject, but others won't necessarily agree with it. Your job is to come up with two, three, or more good reasons that could get the reader to share your point of view.

There are two main ways to help get readers to see something the way you do. One way is to appeal to the reader's "head," or sense of logic. "Logical reasons" can be facts, such as statistics:

> **Almost 95% of all Americans own at least one TV.**

They can be quotations from an expert on a subject:

> **In support of female goalie Manon Rheaume, *Tampa Tribune* sportswriter Tom Jones said, "She did a respectable job. She played as well as any goaltender would have."**

They can be examples from your own or other people's experience:

> **I've found that stores are less crowded at night.**

Another way to persuade readers is to appeal to their "heart," or emotions. The following paragraphs are from "A Plea for the Chimps," a persuasive essay against using animals in experiments. Study how Jane Goodall, a famous expert on chimpanzees, describes what she saw in a lab housing chimps used in experiments.

> **A . . . female rocked from side to side, sealed off from the outside world behind the glass doors of her metal isolation chamber. She was in semidarkness. All she could hear was the . . . roar of air rushing through vents into her prison. . . .**
>
> **I shall be haunted forever by her eyes, and by the eyes of the other infant chimpanzees I saw that day. Have you ever looked into the eyes of a person who . . . has given up . . . ? I once saw a little African boy, whose whole family had been killed during the fighting in Burundi. He too looked out at the world, unseeing, from dull, blank eyes.**

Goodall's description is designed to make readers feel sorry for the chimpanzees. Notice that she uses many emotion-packed words: *prison, haunted, dull, blank*. She also compares the feelings of an infant chimp and a child to help readers relate to the chimps. By touching readers' hearts, Goodall hopes to make them care about her topic and give her their support.

Emotional appeals can be powerful. But it's important to use them in a responsible way. Using unfair emotional appeals, such as name-calling or personal attacks, usually backfires. In the end, they make the writer, rather than the object of the attack, look bad.

Exercise 2

For each statement of opinion, write two reasons why someone might hold the opinion. Use one logical reason and one emotional reason. Follow the example.

▶ Crime is our country's biggest problem.

Logic: _The newspaper says serious crime rose 12% last year._

Emotion: _Decent, law-abiding people are being gunned down._

1. All of our nation's children must be given the opportunity to get a good education.

Logic: _____

Emotion: _____

2. Drugs are tearing apart our neighborhoods.

Logic: _____

Emotion: _____

3. It's not good for children to see so much violence on TV.

Logic: _____

Emotion: _____

Answers will vary.

Organizing Ideas: Three Good Patterns

To make the best case you can for your opinion, organize your reasons so that they'll be the most convincing to your reader. In Chapter 6, you learned that you can put examples in any order when they are all equally important. The same is true for the reasons in the body of a persuasive essay. If you feel they're all equally good, you can simply state them one right after the other.

You also learned in Chapter 6 that examples may be organized in order of importance, with the strongest example last. The same is true in persuasive essays. You can save your best reason for last, so that you leave your reader thinking about the strongest point you want to make.

There's a trick you also can use if you think one of your reasons is weaker than the others. You can bury it between two stronger reasons, like a piece of lunchmeat in a sandwich. Look at the difference between the order of importance method and the "sandwich" method.

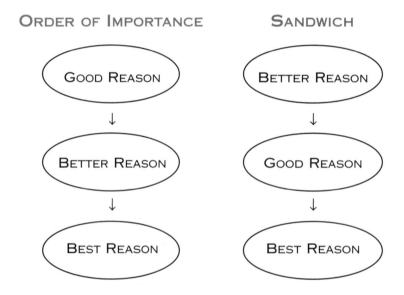

ORDER OF IMPORTANCE   SANDWICH

GOOD REASON   BETTER REASON

↓   ↓

BETTER REASON   GOOD REASON

↓   ↓

BEST REASON   BEST REASON

The sandwich technique allows writers to begin and end with their most convincing reasons. As a result, many writers like to use this pattern of organization in their persuasive essays. (The reasons in the persuasive essay on page 112 are in sandwich order.)

Exercise 3

Underline the opinion statement in each paragraph. Then circle the letter of the type of organization used in the paragraph.

Some Good Advice

I think I know you well enough to say it: that guy's not right for you. You like to go out and dance; he likes to stay in and watch TV. You're good with money and you pay your bills on time; he's always bouncing checks. And you have a steady job. The last time he held a job, Reagan was president.

1. **(a)** equal importance
   (b) order of importance
   (c) sandwich order

Vote for Me!

If you elect me, I'll make this country better. I'll work to keep crime off the streets. I'll improve the nation's health-care system. And I'll make sure that everyone who wants a job can find one.

2. **(a)** equal importance
   (b) order of importance
   (c) sandwich order

Come to the Auto Show

Attend the auto show—there's no better way to spend a Saturday! See all the hot, new cars. Pick up your free bag of popcorn. Best of all, win a brand new Chevy Blazer!

3. **(a)** equal importance
   (b) order of importance
   (c) sandwich order

Check your answers on page 218.

IN YOUR JOURNAL

Pick a controversial issue—one that people are likely to have different opinions about, such as the death penalty or abortion. State your opinion, and make a list of reasons to back it up. Then rate your reasons. Label the strongest reason *1*, the second strongest reason *2*, and so on. Try reading your reasons in different orders—first in order of importance and then in sandwich order. Which order is more effective? Why?

Read Persuasive Essays

You've studied three elements of a persuasive essay: the statement of opinion, supporting reasons, and ways to organize reasons. Look for these elements as you read the following essays.

What is your opinion about the death penalty? Here, two young journalists take opposing sides on the issue. With whom do you agree?

Why I Am for the Death Penalty

by Richard Myers

(1) While there are many powerful arguments against the death penalty, I believe it is justifiable in many cases.

(2) It is a powerful **deterrent**[1], particularly to the people sentenced to death. They will never again commit the crime they were convicted of.

(3) The death penalty also serves as a deterrent to people who may be considering killing. If it is a well-known and well-publicized fact that anyone convicted of planning and committing a murder will end up in the electric chair, it may force someone to have second thoughts.

(4) Another argument for the death penalty is the very high cost of housing, feeding, and guarding dangerous criminals in a penitentiary. While they are in the penitentiary, they also pose a risk to other people in prison, many of whom have never been convicted of a violent act. If prisons are really designed to help convicted people reform and return to society, then keeping convicted murderers in the same place is harmful.

(5) There is also a moral argument for the death penalty. Some people have committed crimes so terrible that they do, in fact, owe society their life.

(6) U.S. law is built around the belief that it is better that ten guilty men go free than one innocent man go to prison. I agree that use of the death penalty should be limited to specific crimes that have been particularly brutal. Convicted murderers should have the right to pursue appeals throughout the system or gain a new trial when new evidence comes to light. It is possible that other circumstances would also limit the use of the death penalty.

(7) But if someone has run out of appeals and the conviction still stands, a jury should have the right to decide that the person owes society his or her life because of the brutality of the crime.

---

[1]**deterrent:** something that prevents an action from occurring

Why I Oppose the Death Penalty

by Steve Cline

(1) The death penalty does not benefit society in any way.

(2) The most common argument in favor of the death penalty is that it makes other people think twice before killing someone. However, no study has ever proven that the death penalty reduces the number of murders committed. In a 1988 study run by the United Nations not a single country could produce evidence that the death penalty deterred crime.

(3) The threat of death does not work because most murderers do not consider the consequences of their action. In many cases, the person committing murder is mentally disturbed and unable to think clearly. In other cases, the murderer may mistakenly believe that he or she will not be caught. In all of these situations, the decision to kill is not based on logic. The thought of the death penalty would not even cross the murderer's mind.

(4) The old saying "an eye for an eye" is also used to justify killing those who kill. But is it really the most suitable punishment? The impact of a murder is long lasting. The punishment for such a crime should be just as lasting. As punishment, the death penalty is over in a moment. A life prison sentence, however, continues to punish for years and years.

(5) There are also practical reasons for opposing the death penalty. First, studies show that minority criminals are given the death penalty and are actually put to death in higher proportions than white criminals. As activist Frank Chapman put it, "For 48 percent of the death row population in our country to be Black is clearly practicing **genocide**[1] when you consider that Afro-Americans are only 12 percent of our population."

(6) Second, those put on death row often wait years for their sentence to be carried out because of costly and time-consuming appeals. The argument that it is cheaper to carry out the death penalty than to house a prisoner for life often becomes **moot**[2], because the prisoner frequently dies a natural death behind bars while waiting.

(7) Perhaps the most important argument against the death penalty is that it reduces the value of all human life. Society should not punish a murderer by committing what amounts to the same act. True, it removes the murderer from the streets. But so does a life sentence in prison.

(8) When a prisoner is killed, it is with everyone's consent. We are all a part of the killing even if we never throw the switch for the electric chair or strap a prisoner into the gas chamber. The death penalty involves us all in a terrible, unjustified act.

---

[1] **genocide:** the murder of a cultural or racial group   [2] **moot:** open to question

Check Your Understanding

Answer each question about "Why I Am for the Death Penalty" and "Why I Oppose the Death Penalty." Look back at the essays if you need to.

1. The introduction to each essay clearly states the writer's opinion about the death penalty. Copy each writer's statement of opinion.

   _____

   _____

2. What method of organization does Richard Myers use in his essay? Circle the letter.

   (a) order of importance

   (b) sandwich order

3. In "Why I Oppose the Death Penalty," Steve Cline says the death penalty does not prevent others from killing. What are two reasons he gives for feeling this way?

   _____

   _____

4. Does the following statement appeal to the reader's sense of logic or emotion? Circle the letter.

   In a 1988 study run by the United Nations not a single country could produce evidence that the death penalty deterred crime.

   (a) logic

   (b) emotion

5. Does the following statement appeal to the reader's sense of logic or emotion? Circle the letter.

   When a prisoner is killed, it is with everyone's consent. We are all a part of the killing even if we never throw the switch for the electric chair or strap a prisoner into the gas chamber. The death penalty involves us all in a terrible, unjustified act.

   (a) logic

   (b) emotion

Check your answers on page 218.

■ | Write a Persuasive Essay

Prewriting: Selecting a Topic and Purpose

You've just read two persuasive essays on the death penalty. **Write your own persuasive essay about a topic that's important to you.**

Think of a subject you feel strongly about. What changes in the world would you like to see made? Or what would you like to change someone's mind about? The topic you choose could be

- ▶ Bilingual education
- ▶ Unions
- ▶ National health insurance
- ▶ Movie ratings
- ▶ Legalized gambling
- ▶ Space travel
- ▶ Marrying young
- ▶ Gun control

Below are some ideas to help you get started. Choose *one* of these topics or use one of your own. You may also want to check your journal. See if you expressed an opinion you would like to write about in an essay.

- ▶ Why I am for (or against) bilingual education
- ▶ Why I am for (or against) unions
- ▶ Why I am for (or against) national health insurance
- ▶ Why I am for (or against) the movie rating system
- ▶ Why I am for (or against) legalized gambling
- ▶ Why I am for (or against) space travel
- ▶ Why I am for (or against) marrying young
- ▶ Why I am for (or against) stricter gun control

Write your topic below.

Topic:

_____

Prewriting: Developing Your Topic

Now that you have your topic, you need to develop it by thinking of reasons to support your opinion. You may appeal to logic, emotions, or a combination of the two.

Freewriting is a good way to get ideas for a persuasive essay. (You learned about freewriting in Chapter 2.) Here are a student's freewriting notes. His topic was lotteries.

It's a waste of time. Your chances of winning are so tiny. They say money goes to the schools. So how come they still need money? Lottery isn't helping enough. People waste money they should spend on their families. Seems like there should be a better way to get money!

On the lines below, freewrite about the topic you chose.

Prewriting: Organizing Your Ideas

Finishing prewriting by organizing your ideas.

▶ **Write a main idea sentence.**

The sentence should clearly state your opinion about the topic.

Main idea sentence: _____

_____

▶ **Now, group your supporting reasons.**
Draw a cluster for each reason you want to use in your essay. Connect the reason to your main idea sentence. Follow the student example.

Lotteries should be outlawed

Aren't helping schools that much.

Waste of money. Chances of winning too small.

People waste money they need for their families

▶ **Decide what order to put your reasons in.** Are some of the arguments stronger than others? You may want to organize your arguments by order of importance or in sandwich order. Are all of your arguments equally strong? In this case, the order is up to you. Decide which method of organization you will use. **Write the order below.**

Order: _____

If you want, number your examples to show the order you want them in.

Drafting

The next stage of the writing process is drafting. During this stage, you use your prewriting plan to write. Remember that a first draft is just a first try. You'll have a chance to improve your writing when you revise and edit.

Using your plan, write a first draft on the topic of your choice. If you need more space, write on another piece of paper.

INCLUDE A
CLEARLY
STATED
OPINION
IN THE
INTRODUCTION.

_____

_____

_____

_____

_____

_____

_____

_____

USE A
TRANSITION
TO
INTRODUCE
EACH
REASON.

_____

_____

_____

_____

_____

_____

_____

_____

END BY
SUMMING UP.

_____

Revising

Your next step is to evaluate your draft, alone or with a partner. First, do the Revision Warm-Up. Then use the Revision Checklist to revise your draft.

Revision Warm-Up

Follow the directions below.

1. Add a time-order transition at the beginning of paragraphs 2, 3, and 4 to show that a new reason is coming up. (A list of these transitions is on page 68).
2. Add a concluding paragraph that includes a restatement of the main idea.

Lotteries Are a Waste

I think lotteries should be outlawed, or at least not allowed every day, for several reasons.

They're a waste of money, because your chances of winning are actually very small. I know people who like to play every now and then; I say, play for fun, but don't count on the money to pay your bills.

They say the money goes for schools, but it seems like the schools still always need money. Maybe they should do a better job managing the money they have. At any rate, lotteries clearly aren't the answer to school funding.

People spend money they need for other things—groceries, kids, clothes—on lottery tickets. They're a temptation that many of us just don't need.

Check your answers on page 218.

✍ Revision Checklist

Yes	No	
☐	☐	1. Does the introduction clearly state an opinion?
☐	☐	2. Does the body include reasons to support the opinion?
☐	☐	3. Are the reasons clear?
☐	☐	4. Are the reasons organized effectively?
☐	☐	5. Does the essay have a concluding paragraph?
☐	☐	6. Does the conclusion help sum up the main idea?

Editing

The last stage of the writing process is editing. During this stage, you look for and correct errors in grammar, mechanics, and usage.

Do the Editing Exercise. Then look for and correct any noun, pronoun, verb, adjective and adverb, and sentence structure errors in your draft. Also look for other errors. If possible, work with a partner.

Editing Exercise: Punctuation

Twelve commas, one semicolon, and two colons are missing from the letter. Add them where needed.

September 1 19––

Miss Georgene Curtis

1920 South Grove

Lincolnville KY 40272

Dear Miss Curtis

For the past several months you have been enjoying *Sportswrite* America's leading sports magazine. But now Miss Curtis your subscription is about to expire. You have only until October 1 19–– to take action. Don't let your subscription lapse! Just $12.99 buys you another twelve months of the best sports reporting.

Don't miss out on wonderful stories like the following

▶ "Is Baseball Doomed?"
▶ "You Pick 'Em: The Top Ten NFL QBs of All Time"
▶ "Foreman: Back in the Ring Again?"

The most insightful stories the most accurate predictions the most complete statistics are yours once again for the asking. Just fill out the enclosed postcard we'll bill you later. (You can if you prefer charge your subscription now.)

Check your answers on page 218.

PART II
GRAMMAR

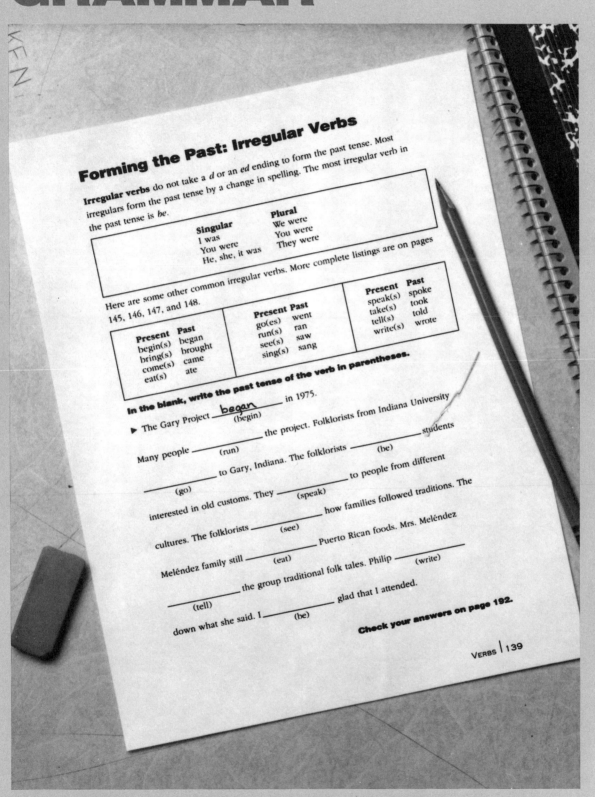

Forming the Past: Irregular Verbs

Irregular verbs do not take a *d* or an *ed* ending to form the past tense. Most irregulars form the past tense by a change in spelling. The most irregular verb in the past tense is *be*.

Singular	Plural
I was	We were
You were	You were
He, she, it was	They were

Here are some other common irregular verbs. More complete listings are on pages 145, 146, 147, and 148.

Present	Past
begin(s)	began
bring(s)	brought
come(s)	came
eat(s)	ate

Present	Past
go(es)	went
run(s)	ran
see(s)	saw
sing(s)	sang

Present	Past
speak(s)	spoke
take(s)	took
tell(s)	told
write(s)	wrote

In the blank, write the past tense of the verb in parentheses.

▶ The Gary Project __began__ in 1975.
(begin)

Many people _____ the project. Folklorists from Indiana University
(run)

_____ to Gary, Indiana. The folklorists _____ students
(go)   (be)

interested in old customs. They _____ to people from different
(speak)

cultures. The folklorists _____ how families followed traditions. The
(see)

Meléndez family still _____ Puerto Rican foods. Mrs. Meléndez
(eat)

_____ the group traditional folk tales. Philip _____
(tell)   (write)

down what she said. I _____ glad that I attended.
(be)

Check your answers on page 192.

CHAPTER 9 | NOUNS

Identifying Nouns

A **noun** is a word that names a person, place, or thing.

Persons:	Mr. Chung, Dan, Aunt Amy, neighbor, politician, child
Places:	store, Alaska, Rain Avenue, yard, jail, home
Things:	screwdriver, kitten, door, friendship, hope, toy

PART A

Underline the nouns in each sentence.

▶ <u>Carlos</u> and <u>Rita Esquivel</u> are <u>husband</u> and <u>wife</u>.

1. The man and woman work as chefs in Chicago.

2. Carlos makes pastry at the Star Café.

3. Rita prepares sauces for a restaurant on Oak Street.

4. Carlos and Rita enjoy their jobs.

5. Diners like the food.

6. The man is often asked to bake cakes for parties.

7. The woman adds special spices to her sauces.

8. The two cooks share a dream for the future.

9. The Esquivels want to open their own place in a few years.

10. The restaurant should be a success.

PART B

Write the name of the person, place, or thing in parentheses.

(your street)   1._____

(your favorite restaurant)   2._____

(your city or town)   3._____

(your best friend)   4._____

(your favorite food)   5._____

Check your answers on page 219.

Capitalizing Nouns I

Capitalize **proper nouns**—specific names of persons, places, and things. Do not capitalize **common nouns**—general names of persons, places, and things.

Proper nouns:	Oprah Winfrey, Horton Hotel, Korean War
Common nouns:	woman, hotel, war

Be sure to capitalize all main parts of a proper noun.

▶ the Midville Museum of Natural History

Capitalize job and family titles that come directly before a name and are considered to be part of the name.

▶ Doctor Wong, President Roosevelt, Aunt Marie

Capitalize the proper nouns in each sentence.

▶ My son Lee is a student at Ball State University.

1. Lee went on a vacation to new orleans, louisiana.

2. His brother luis goes to tulane university.

3. Lee was amazed by the size of lake pontchartrain.

4. Luis took lee to bourbon street.

5. It is in the french quarter, my favorite part of the city.

6. After lunch, the two walked to jackson square.

7. Then, the boys caught the streetcar to meet uncle jerome.

8. Uncle jerome was talking to congresswoman jones.

9. The congresswoman left to go back to the hilton hotel.

10. The family went to hear buddy guy, a blues singer.

11. Lee had first heard guy in chicago.

12. The family also saw a great jazz band at preservation hall.

13. Later, the boys went to their uncle's house on paris road.

14. Aunt jana served fish she'd caught in the mississippi river.

Check your answers on page 219.

Capitalizing Nouns II

Capitalize days of the week and months of the year.
▶ <u>M</u>onday, <u>F</u>riday, <u>J</u>anuary, <u>F</u>ebruary

Do not capitalize the seasons of the year.
▶ spring, summer, winter, fall

Capitalize specific holidays.
▶ <u>E</u>aster, <u>T</u>hanksgiving, the <u>F</u>ourth of <u>J</u>uly

PART A

Capitalize the proper noun or nouns in each sentence.

▶ Many holidays should occur on **M**ondays or **F**ridays.

1. If thanksgiving were on monday, all the cooking could be done over the weekend.

2. Trick-or-treating on friday night would make halloween easier on parents.

3. Couples could sleep late on saturday after a valentine's day date on friday night.

4. I also wish new year's eve were in may.

5. It is too cold in january to celebrate.

6. The heat of summer might be better for presidents' day.

7. Of course, the cold of winter is perfect for christmas.

8. But birthdays on december 25 should be banned.

PART B

Complete the questionnaire. Be sure to capitalize correctly.

Your address:_____
(street)

_____
(city)   (state)   (ZIP)

Your doctor's name:_____
(first)   (last)

Days you work or go to school:_____

Check your answers on page 219.

Identifying Plural Nouns

A **plural noun** names more than one person, place, or thing. Form the plural of most nouns by adding an *s* ending.

▶ each girl—two girl<u>s</u>, this room—those room<u>s</u>

Signal words can tell you if a noun should be singular or plural. Some common singular signal words are *one, a, an, each, every, a single, this,* and *that.* Some common plural signal words are *two, both, several, many, these,* and *those.*

▶ It took <u>three fathers</u> to move <u>that table</u>.

Context—the way a word is used in combination with other words—also can tell you if a noun should be singular or plural.

▶ The <u>boys</u> on the <u>team</u> stay late to practice.

In the sentence above, you can tell that *boys* should be plural because a team consists of more than one boy.

PART A

Circle *S* if the underlined noun is singular or *P* if it is plural.

S Ⓟ ▶ both <u>tables</u>

S P **1.** a <u>plate</u>

S P **2.** four <u>cakes</u>

S P **3.** every <u>glass</u>

S P **4.** several <u>eggs</u>

S P **5.** many <u>desserts</u>

PART B

Underline and correct the plural error in each sentence.

       boys
▶ The two <u>boy</u> set the table.

Hsu put out a stack of napkin for the whole family. Then Mr. Nurachi brought in several bowl of beans. The mother placed a pair of chopstick by each plate. All member of the family sat down to eat.

Check your answers on page 219.

Spelling Regular Plurals

Use these guidelines to spell the plural of **regular nouns**.

Form the plural of nouns that end in *s, sh, ch, x,* and *z* by adding an *es* ending.

▶ one dre<u>ss</u>—two dre<u>sses</u>, a sa<u>sh</u>—several sa<u>shes</u>

Form the plural of nouns that end in a consonant and a *y* by changing *y* to *i* and adding *es.*

▶ a bab<u>y</u>—many bab<u>ies</u>, one cit<u>y</u>—many cit<u>ies</u>

In some cases, nouns ending in *f* or *fe* form the plural with an *s* ending. In other cases, the plural is formed by changing the *f* or *fe* to *v* and adding *es.*

▶ this sa<u>fe</u>—these sa<u>fes</u>, a kni<u>fe</u>—both kni<u>ves</u>

Form the plural of nouns ending in a vowel and an *o* by adding *s.* Form the plural of most nouns ending in a consonant and an *o* by adding *es.*

▶ one ster<u>eo</u>—two ster<u>eos</u>, a pota<u>to</u>—those pota<u>toes</u>

Underline the correct plural form in parentheses.

▶ Cesar Chavez is one of my (heros, <u>heroes</u>).

1. His work changed the (lifes, lives) of many migrant workers.

2. With the help of union (attorneys, attornies), Chavez organized a strike against grape growers.

3. Many American (familys, families) refused to buy grapes.

4. People left lettuce on grocery store (shelfs, shelves).

5. (Churchs, Churches) across the nation supported the boycott.

6. Now many migrant workers, such as those who pick (tomatos, tomatoes), have contracts.

7. What are your (beliefs, believes) about boycotts?

8. Should people boycott (companys, companies) they dislike?

Check your answers on page 219.

Spelling Irregular Plurals

Irregular nouns don't follow the rules for forming noun plurals. Use these guidelines to spell the plurals of irregular nouns.

For some irregular nouns, the plural form is the same as the singular form.
▶ a deer—several deer, one fish—two fish

Some irregular nouns have only a plural form.
▶ scissors, eyeglasses, pants, clothes

The plural of some irregular nouns is formed by changing the spelling of the noun.
▶ one wom<u>a</u>n—two wom<u>e</u>n, every child—many child<u>ren</u>
▶ that t<u>oo</u>th—these t<u>ee</u>th, a m<u>ouse</u>—several m<u>ice</u>
▶ one p<u>erson</u>—both p<u>eople</u> (or person<u>s</u>)

Write the plural of the noun in parentheses.

▶ A group of ___*children*___ made a mural.
   (child)

1. They used _____ to cut animal shapes.
                (scissors)

2. They drew pictures of birds and _____ .
                                    (fish)

3. Some kids painted pictures of _____.
                                  (mouse)

4. One boy drew only the animals'_____ .
                                    (tooth)

5. More paint got on _____ than on paper.
              (clothes)

6. Two kids ruined their shirts and _____ .
                                    (pants)

7. Many _____ came to see the mural.
        (person)

8. The two _____ who ran the school were proud.
           (woman)

Check your answers on page 219.

Forming Singular Possessives

A **possessive noun** shows ownership or relationship. Use these guidelines to form **singular possessives**.

Form the possessive of singular nouns by adding an apostrophe (') and an *s*.

▶ John<u>'s</u> book was missing. (The book belongs to John.)

▶ The man<u>'s</u> wife called. (The wife of the man called.)

Even when a singular noun ends in *s*, add *'s* to form the possessive.

▶ Mr. Santos<u>'s</u> book is on the table.

PART A

Make each underlined noun singular possessive.

▶ Mrs. Pallas just read a new <u>writers</u> second novel.

1. The <u>authors</u> name is Amy Tan.

2. <u>Tans</u> book is about a mother and daughter.

3. The <u>mothers</u> part of the story is set in China.

4. Mrs. <u>Pallass</u> favorite chapter is at the end of the book.

5. The older woman reveals a secret about her <u>daughters</u> past.

6. The <u>novels</u> title is *The Kitchen God's Wife.*

PART B

Using a possessive noun, rewrite the phrase in parentheses. Be sure to put the apostrophe where it belongs.

▶ ____the writer's house____

(the house of the writer)

1. _____

(the plot of the novel)

2. _____

(the interest of the reader)

3. _____

(the cover of the book)

Check your answers on page 220.

Forming Plural Possessives

Form the possessive of regular plural nouns by adding an apostrophe (') after the *s*.

▶ the twins' room

▶ the Sanchezes' apartment

▶ many companies' problems

PART A

Make each underlined noun plural possessive.

▶ Our landlords often ignore their renters' troubles.

1. Last night we held a tenants meeting.

2. We all met in the Golds apartment.

3. Mrs. Gold made a list of all families complaints.

4. The Schwartzes complaint was about their plumbing.

5. The Schramms complained about their windows broken latches.

6. The Smiths problem was a broken front door lock.

7. I said that our two bedrooms electrical sockets are unsafe.

8. Maybe a letter will get those landlords attention.

PART B

Using a possessive noun, rewrite the phrase in parentheses. Be sure to put the apostrophe where it belongs.

▶ _the ladies' hats_
(the hats of the ladies)

1. _____
(the cases of the attorneys)

2. _____
(the products of several companies)

3. _____
(the complaints of the wives)

Check your answers on page 220.

Forming Irregular Possessives

To form the possessive of plural nouns that do not end in *s*, add an apostrophe (') and an *s*.

▶ men's fashions

▶ children's books

▶ people's preferences

PART A

Using a possessive noun, rewrite the phrase in parentheses. Be sure to put the apostrophe where it belongs.

▶ _the men's job_
(the job of the men)

1. _____
(the boats of the fishermen)

2. _____
(the toys of the children)

3. _____
(the uniforms of the women)

4. _____
(the tracks of the two deer)

5. _____
(the tails of those mice)

6. _____
(the choice of the people)

PART B

This is a review of the possessive noun rules. Underline and add an apostrophe to the possessive noun in each sentence.

▶ My <u>town's</u> public library is excellent.

The librarys collection of books and magazines is impressive. The friendly staff works hard to meet peoples needs. The childrens room has books, magazines, tapes, records, and computers. The room has won many parents praise.

Check your answers on page 220.

Chapter 9 Review

This exercise is a review of the main rules you have studied in this chapter. Underline and correct the noun error in each sentence.

► I just read Steve <u>Smith's</u> new book about 1968.

1. Are you old enough to remember the Vietnam war?

2. My brother bill was wounded there.

3. Some of his buddys also were wounded.

4. They encountered ambushs in the jungle.

5. Bill came home on the tuesday just before Labor Day.

6. Bills brother-in-law threw a party.

7. That Fall, Bill started attending junior college.

8. In 1968, womens clothing stores featured the miniskirt.

9. Mens' hairstyles were wild compared to styles of the past.

10. Kids listened to rock music on their stereoes.

11. Many kids dream was to become a rock musician.

12. Several rock group had hits with antiwar songs.

13. Students were protesting lifes lost in the war.

14. Some peoples staged demonstrations against the draft.

15. Antiwar activists were angry with president Johnson.

16. Several protest turned violent.

17. In 1968, Columbia university was hit with protests.

18. That summer, demonstrators marched in downtown chicago.

19. They also staged demonstrations in Lincoln park.

20. Many americans were upset about the protests.

Check your answers on page 220.

CHAPTER 10 | PRONOUNS

Identifying Pronouns

A **pronoun** is a word that can replace a noun.

▶ The <u>lock</u> is broken. I'll fix <u>it</u>. (*It* replaces *lock*.)

First person pronouns refer to the person who is speaking in a sentence. **Second person** pronouns refer to the person being spoken to. **Third person** pronouns refer to the person or thing spoken about. Pronouns can be singular or plural.

	Singular	**Plural**
First person	I, me, my, mine, myself	we, us, our, ours, ourselves
Second person	you, your, yours, yourself	you, your, yours, yourselves
Third person	he, him, his, himself she, her, hers, herself it, its, itself	they, them, their, theirs, themselves

Underline the pronoun or pronouns in each sentence.

▶ <u>My</u> husband has <u>his</u> own business.

1. He repairs motorcycles when they break down.

2. His store also sells new motorcycles.

3. You may have seen the newspaper ads.

4. One of them ran yesterday.

5. My assistant and I take care of sales.

6. She is learning how to do repairs too.

7. Her brother has already taught himself how to do repairs.

8. I myself wouldn't mind learning about them.

9. We all are proud of our shop.

10. It is small, but our work is good.

Check your answers on page 220.

Using Subject Pronouns

Subject pronouns take the place of subject nouns. A **subject** is the person, place, or thing a sentence is about.

▶ <u>Ed</u> called. <u>He</u> left a message. (*He* replaces the subject noun *Ed*.)

▶ <u>Sewing</u> is easy. <u>It</u> is fun. (*It* replaces the subject noun *sewing*.)

The subject pronouns are *I, you, he, she, it, we,* and *they.*

PART A

In the parentheses, write the pronoun that correctly replaces the underlined subject noun or nouns.

▶ <u>Linda</u> (_she_) is reading a new book.

1. <u>Tony Hillerman</u> (_____) wrote the mystery novel.

2. <u>The novel</u> (_____) is about a Navaho detective, Jim Chee.

3. <u>Jim Chee</u> (_____) investigates a woman's disappearance.

4. <u>The woman</u> (_____) knew a secret about some thieves.

5. <u>The thieves</u> (_____) were afraid the woman would tell.

6. <u>Linda and I</u> (_____) think the thieves killed the woman.

7. Do <u>you and Al</u> (_____) know how the novel ends?

8. <u>Guessing the ending</u> (_____) is part of the fun.

PART B

Write a sentence for each pronoun in parentheses.

▶ (we) __We are planning a party.__

1. (I) _____

2. (she) _____

3. (they) _____

4. (it) _____

Check your answers on page 220.

Using Object Pronouns I

Object pronouns take the place of **object nouns** in a sentence. The **direct object** receives the action in a sentence.

▶ Tim kissed <u>her</u>. (Who received the kiss? *Her*)

The **indirect object** receives the direct object.

▶ She gave <u>him</u> her love. (Who received her love? *Him*)

The object pronouns are *me, you, him, her, it, us,* and *them.*

PART A

In the parentheses, write the pronoun that correctly replaces the underlined object noun or nouns.

▶ I first heard <u>Louis Armstrong</u> (_**him**_) play jazz in 1964.

1. A recording of "Hello Dolly!" brought <u>Armstrong</u> (_____) to my attention.

2. My parents bought <u>my brother and me</u> (_____) the record.

3. I played <u>that record and others</u> (_____) for Jess and Tom.

4. They hadn't heard <u>jazz</u> (_____) before.

5. Tom's mother asked <u>Jess, Tom, and me</u> (_____) why we liked jazz.

6. We couldn't give <u>Mrs. Sanders</u> (_____) an answer.

7. So we asked <u>Tom's mom</u> (_____) to listen to our records.

8. She said that she liked <u>the songs</u> (_____).

9. I'll lend <u>you and your friends</u> (_____) the records.

10. I'm sure that you'll enjoy <u>the music</u> (_____).

PART B
Write a sentence for each pronoun in parentheses.

▶ (me) _George taught me how to play the piano._

1. (him) _____

2. (her) _____

3. (us) _____

Check your answers on page 220.

Using Object Pronouns II

Pronouns that follow prepositions also take the object form. These pronouns are called **objects of the preposition**.

▶ Give it <u>to me</u>. (*Me* is the object of the preposition *to*.)

Common Prepositions			
about	beside	from	to
after	between	in	toward
against	by	near	under
at	except	on	with
behind	for	over	without

PART A

In the parentheses, write the pronoun that correctly replaces the underlined noun object or objects of the preposition.

▶ Mr. West will take a picture of <u>the club members</u> (*them*).

1. We'll start the picture taking without <u>Mary</u> (_____).

2. Martha, will you stand over by <u>Bill</u> (_____) ?

3. John, please sit in <u>the first chair</u> (_____).

4. Della, you should move near <u>Harry and Bill</u> (_____).

5. Mrs. Romero, please stand beside <u>Ellen and me</u> (_____).

6. Take Mr. Samms with <u>Fred and you</u> (_____).

7. Will someone turn the light toward <u>the last row</u> (_____) ?

8. Everyone smile and look at <u>the camera</u> (_____).

PART B

This is a review of the object pronoun rules. Underline and correct the pronoun error in each sentence.

▶ Our instructor gave <u>we</u> a writing assignment.
               us

He asked I to read my essay aloud. He also asked Yolanda to read her essay to he.

Then he gave she constructive criticism.

Check your answers on page 221.

Using Pronouns in Compounds

Subjects joined by *and, nor,* or *or* are called **compound subjects**. Objects joined by *and, nor,* or *or* are called **compound objects**. A pronoun in a compound subject takes the subject form.

▶ Okei and (I, me) work at a computer store.

A pronoun in a compound object takes the object form.

▶ Lunch is at 1:30 for Okei and (I, me).

If you have trouble deciding which form to use, read each part of the compound separately.

▶ Okei works at a computer store. I work at a computer store.

▶ Lunch is at 1:30 for Okei. Lunch is at 1:30 for me.

PART A

Underline the correct pronoun in parentheses.

▶ Have you and (she, her) tried the new Korean restaurant?

1. Okei and (I, me) went there last week.

2. (She, Her) and I had hot rice dishes.

3. The owner's wife waited on my friend and (I, me).

4. We told John and (he, him) about the place.

5. John asked Roger and (we, us) to meet there yesterday.

6. (We, Us) and (they, them) ate a spicy soup and seafood.

7. Roger and (he, him) also ordered a special tea.

8. I thanked Okei and (they, them) for a pleasant meal.

PART B

Underline and correct the compound subject or object pronoun error in each sentence.

▶ Mr. Takei and her like Mexican food.
       she

Neither their children nor them know how to cook it. So the children sometimes take he and her out to eat. You and me should go with them sometime.

Check your answers on page 221.

Using Possessive Pronouns I

Possessive pronouns are used to show ownership or relationship.

▶ <u>My</u> dog chased <u>your</u> cat into <u>their</u> yard.

The possessive pronouns are *my, your, his, her, its, our,* and *their.* Do not confuse the pronouns in each of these pairs: *your—you're, their—they're, its—it's.*
Your is a possessive pronoun. *You're* is short for *you are.*

▶ <u>You're</u> crazy about <u>your</u> cat.

Their is a possessive pronoun. *They're* is short for *they are.*

▶ <u>They're</u> angry that the dog dug up <u>their</u> yard.

Its is a possessive pronoun. *It's* is short for *it is.*

▶ <u>It's</u> too bad that the cat hurt <u>its</u> paw.

PART A

Underline the correct pronoun in parentheses.

▶ Do (<u>your,</u> you're) parents live close to you?

1. Dino and Mikel often write to (their, they're) mother.

2. (They're, Their) planning to visit her this summer.

3. (Its, It's) too expensive to make long-distance phone calls.

4. The phone company keeps raising (its, it's) rates.

5. How often do you see (your, you're) parents?

6. (Your, You're) lucky if you can visit them once a week.

PART B

Write a sentence for each pronoun in parentheses.

▶ (my)   *My vacation starts in a few days.*

1. (your)   _____

2. (his)   _____

3. (its)   _____

4. (their)   _____

Check your answers on page 221.

Using Possessive Pronouns II

Some possessive pronouns can stand alone. These pronouns are *mine, yours, his, hers, its, ours,* and *theirs.*

▶ That car is <u>hers</u>. You can borrow <u>mine</u>.

Mine is the only one of these pronouns that does not end in *s*. Notice that none of the pronouns takes an apostrophe.

PART A

Underline the pronoun in parentheses that correctly replaces the underlined words.

▶ Is your dentist in the same building as <u>my dentist?</u>
(<u>mine</u>, mines)

1. <u>My dentist</u> is Dr. Carmen Rivera, a family friend.
(Mine, Mines)

2. Do you remember the phone number of <u>your dentist?</u>
(your, yours)

3. <u>Dr. Rivera's office</u> is on the top floor of the complex.
(Hers, Her's)

4. <u>The other dentists' offices</u> are on the first floor.
(Theirs, Their's)

5. If you don't like your dentist, try <u>our family's dentist</u>.
(our, ours)

PART B

In the parentheses, write the possessive pronoun that correctly replaces the underlined words.

▶ I think this car is <u>Mrs. Garcia's</u> (*hers*).

1. I know it isn't <u>the Jones family's car</u> (_____).

2. Their car looks like <u>the car I own</u> (_____).

3. This one looks more like <u>Jim's</u> (_____).

4. May I borrow <u>your car</u> (_____) ?

Check your answers on page 221.

Using Reflexive Pronouns

A **reflexive pronoun** directs the action expressed by the verb back to the subject.

▶ He taught himself to play guitar.

▶ The cat groomed itself.

Singular reflexive pronouns end in *self*. Plurals end in *selves*.

Singular	**Plural**
myself	ourselves
yourself	yourselves
himself, herself, itself	themselves

Do not use a reflexive pronoun when a subject or object pronoun is needed.

Incorrect: He wants Don and yourself to help.

Correct: He wants Don and you to help.

Do not use *hisself* for *himself* or *theirselves* for *themselves*.

Underline the correct pronoun form in parentheses.

▶ The Bozarths pride (theirselves, themselves) on their ability to do home repairs.

1. I would hurt (me, myself) if I did something like that.

2. Don Bozarth taught (hisself, himself) about plumbing.

3. The kids put (theirselves, themselves) to work painting.

4. Beth told Mr. Silvera and (me, myself) about it yesterday.

5. The Bozarths say the house is practically rebuilding (itself, itselfs).

6. Mr. Silvera and (I, myself) are going over there.

7. Why don't Ellen and (you, yourself) come with us?

8. Get (yourselfs, yourselves) ready.

Check your answers on page 221.

Using Demonstrative Pronouns

Demonstrative pronouns (*this, that, these, those*) are used to point out persons or things. *This* is singular. *These* is plural. *This* and *these* refer to people and things that are nearby or close in time.

▶ <u>These</u> presents I'm holding are yours.

▶ <u>This</u> past year has been good to me.

That and *those* point out persons or things that are farther away in space or time. *Those* is the plural of *that*.

▶ <u>That</u> house across the street is an eyesore.

▶ <u>Those</u> weeds in the back need to be pulled.

▶ Mario will never forget <u>that</u> awful morning last week.

Do not use the expressions *this here* or *that there*. Do not use *them* in place of *those*.

PART A

Underline the correct pronoun form in parentheses.

▶ (<u>This,</u> This here) is your house, isn't it?

1. Is (that, that there) the address we want?

2. (Them, Those) mechanics didn't seem to know this city.

3. If we're lost, we should go back to (that there, that) first left turn we made.

4. (These, These here) directions are the ones to follow.

5. The street is marked with (this here, this) red arrow.

PART B

Write a sentence for each demonstrative pronoun in parentheses.

▶ (this)   I have a lot to do this week.

1. (that) _____

2. (these) _____

3. (those) _____

Check your answers on page 221.

Chapter 10 Review

This exercise is a review of the main rules you have studied in this chapter. Underline the correct pronoun in parentheses.

▶ Do you enjoy (<u>your</u>, you're) job?

1. Mr. Yung's company should improve (its, it's) daycare plan.

2. (He, Him) has sole custody of two little children.

3. Mr. Yung has taught (hisself, himself) how to care for them.

4. Daycare also is a problem for Delia and (she, her).

5. To (them, they), daycare is an important financial issue.

6. The two women even wrote a letter to (their, they're) bosses.

7. (They, Them) and Mr. Yung should exchange ideas.

8. Frances told (we, us) about another problem.

9. Two men were given promotions that she thinks should have been (hers, her's).

10. She says (those, them) men aren't as qualified as she is.

11. Between you and (I, me), she has a good point.

12. (This here, This) is a serious charge.

13. Ramon and (I, myself) agree.

14. The last complaint is (mine, mine's).

15. My supervisors have claimed that one of my ideas is (their's, theirs).

16. Because of (they, them), I lost a bonus.

17. Has anything like this happened to (you, yourself)?

18. I hear that (its, it's) common.

Check your answers on page 221.

Chapter 11 | VERBS

Identifying Verbs

A **verb** is a word that shows action.

▶ Soldiers <u>fight</u> for their country.

A verb can also show a state of being. The state-of-being verbs are *am, is, are, was, were, be, being,* and *been.*

▶ They <u>were</u> brave.

Verb tenses tell when an action or state of being takes place. Sometimes a **helping verb** is used with a **main verb** to form a verb tense. Some common helping verbs are *has, have, had, am, is, are, was,* and *were.*

▶ The soldiers <u>have left</u> the base.

Underline the verb or verbs in each sentence.

▶ The war in the Persian Gulf <u>raised</u> an old question.

1. What is a woman's role in the military?

2. A handful of women enlisted during World War I.

3. They worked as clerks for Marine headquarters.

4. After the war, these "Marinettes" went home.

5. During World War II, women's reserves were formed.

6. Women have served regularly since World War II.

7. But a 1948 law has banned women from active combat.

8. Many people know about military nurses.

9. But female military personnel do many other tasks.

10. They pilot aircraft and assemble bombs.

11. Now, some women are asking for the right to fight.

12. The armed services face a major issue.

Check your answers on page 222.

Understanding Agreement

The **present tense** is used to show that something happens regularly.

▶ The sun <u>rises</u> in the east and <u>sets</u> in the west.

▶ They <u>sing</u> in the choir every Sunday.

Present tense verbs have to be in **agreement** with their subjects. A verb is in agreement if it is in the correct form for the person and number of the subject.

	Singular	**Plural**
First person	I work	We work
Second person	You work	You work
Third person	He, she, it works	They work

Notice that when the subject of a sentence is *he, she,* or *it,* the verb must end in *s.*

▶ <u>He</u> walk<u>s</u>. <u>She</u> talk<u>s</u>. <u>It</u> bark<u>s</u>.

Underline the correct verb form in parentheses.

▶ We (<u>study</u>, studies) together on Friday nights.

1. Usually we (meet, meets) at Sarah's or my house.

2. She always (serve, serves) fruit and nuts as snacks.

3. I (drive, drives) Yolanda and Mario to the study group.

4. They (live, lives) several miles away.

5. At each meeting, he (quiz, quizzes) us on our lessons.

6. He (catch, catches) our mistakes.

7. They (confuse, confuses) me sometimes.

8. You (start, starts) with us tonight, right?

9. It really (help, helps) all of us.

10. We (learn, learns) a lot from each other.

Check your answers on page 222.

Understanding Subject Nouns

When the subject of a sentence is the pronoun *he, she,* or *it,* the verb must end in *s.* To tell what verb form to use with a **noun subject**, replace the noun with the correct pronoun. In the sentence below, for example, *Maria* can be replaced by *she.* Therefore, *works* is the correct verb form.

▶ Maria (work, <u>works</u>) for an accounting firm.

In the sentence below, *bosses* can be replaced by *they.* Therefore, *think* is the correct verb form.

▶ Her bosses (<u>think</u>, thinks) highly of her.

Write the pronoun that correctly replaces the underlined noun subject. Then underline the correct verb form in parentheses.

▶ <u>Sports figures</u> (<u>get</u>, gets) lots of attention. *they*

1. <u>Michael Jordan</u> (play, plays) for the Chicago Bulls.

2. <u>This team</u> (win, wins) a lot of games.

3. <u>Jordan</u> (make, makes) points for his team.

4. <u>Many fans</u> (watch, watches) the games on TV.

5. <u>My mother</u> (see, sees) Jordan in shoe commercials.

6. <u>The athlete</u> (give, gives) money to a foundation.

7. <u>The Michael Jordan Foundation</u> (support, supports) children's charities.

8. <u>Children</u> (admire, admires) Jordan.

9. <u>The man</u> (set, sets) a good example for other athletes.

10. <u>Some people</u> (call, calls) him the best athlete in the world.

11. <u>This high-shooting fellow</u> (try, tries) hard.

12. <u>My sisters and I</u> (love, loves) to watch him play.

Check your answers on page 222.

Using *Be*, *Have*, and *Do*

The chart shows how to use *be*, *have*, and *do* correctly in the present tense.

	Singular	**Plural**
First person	I am, have, do	We are, have, do
Second person	You are, have, do	You are, have, do
Third person	He is, has, does She is, has, does It is, has, does	They are, have, do

In the blank, write the present tense of the verb in parentheses.

▶ It _____*is*_____ time to play baseball!
(be)

1. Today's game _____ against the Sturgis Stumblers.
(be)

2. Their players _____ really good.
(be)

3. That team _____ a good chance of winning.
(have)

4. Jane Littlefeather _____ their pitcher.
(be)

5. She _____ a mean fast ball.
(have)

6. Jane also _____ their coaching.
(do)

7. I _____ the coach for the Factory Fools.
(be)

8. Wait while I _____ the rest of the lineup.
(do)

9. Carlotta, you _____ first up at bat.
(be)

10. You _____ the best batting average.
(have)

Check your answers on page 222.

Looking at Questions and Compounds

In questions, all or part of the verb often comes before the subject. Make sure that the verb agrees with its subject. In the examples below, notice that the verb *is* agrees with the subject *dictionary* and the verb *do* agrees with the subject *you*.

▶ <u>Is</u> the <u>dictionary</u> on the table?

▶ <u>Do you</u> ever use it?

Compound subjects joined by *and* are plural. They need a verb that agrees with a plural subject.

▶ <u>Gus and Connie are</u> in night school.

When a compound subject is joined by *or* or *nor*, the verb agrees with the subject that is closer to the verb.

▶ Neither the students nor the <u>tutor</u> <u>works</u> on Fridays.

Underline the correct verb form in parentheses.

▶ (Are, <u>Is</u>) illiteracy a problem in your community?

1. (Are, Is) Ut and Anna good at reading?

2. Sam and I (are, is) learning to read.

3. Neither Sam nor his parents (have, has) a diploma.

4. Either he or his wife (are, is) finding out about the GED.

5. (Are, Is) you planning to take the equivalency test?

6. What (are, is) we studying today?

7. (Do, Does) you and he study together?

8. Neither Ut nor Anna (like, likes) to study.

9. Sam and I (worry, worries) about passing the test.

10. What (are, is) your opinion about our chances of passing?

11. Reading and studying (take, takes) time.

12. (Have, Has) you seen the sample test?

Check your answers on page 222.

Forming the Past: Regular Verbs

The **past tense** of a verb shows that something has already happened. Form the past tense of **regular verbs** by adding a *d* or *ed* ending.

▶ All last year, Raul walk<u>ed</u> to work.

▶ After a while, he hat<u>ed</u> the walk.

If you have trouble deciding whether a verb should be in the past tense, watch for **time clues**—words that show when an action occurred. Some past tense time clues are *yesterday, last year,* and *a while ago.*

In the blank, write the past tense of the verb in parentheses.

▶ I __**wondered**__ about the origin of hair straighteners.
     (wonder)

1. Last week, I _____ to research the subject.
     (decide)

2. Yesterday, I _____ about an African-American woman.
     (learn)

3. Years ago, Sarah Breedlove _____ of beating poverty.
     (dream)

4. The sharecropper's daughter _____ at fourteen.
     (marry)

5. For years, she _____ clothes for a living.
     (wash)

6. In 1905, Breedlove _____ her own business.
     (start)

7. She _____ herself Mme. C. J. Walker.
     (rename)

8. Mme. Walker _____ various shampoos and oils.
     (mix)

9. The formulas _____ curly hair.
     (straighten)

10. Her products _____ the way many African-American women wore their hair.
     (change)

Check your answers on page 222.

Forming the Past: Irregular Verbs

Irregular verbs do not take a *d* or an *ed* ending to form the past tense. Most irregulars form the past tense by a change in spelling. The most irregular verb in the past tense is *be*.

Singular	**Plural**
I was	We were
You were	You were
He, she, it was	They were

Here are some other common irregular verbs. More complete listings are on pages 161, 162, 163, and 164.

Present	**Past**	**Present**	**Past**	**Present**	**Past**
begin(s)	began	go(es)	went	speak(s)	spoke
bring(s)	brought	run(s)	ran	take(s)	took
come(s)	came	see(s)	saw	tell(s)	told
eat(s)	ate	sing(s)	sang	write(s)	wrote

In the blank, write the past tense of the verb in parentheses.

▶ The Gary Project _____**began**_____ in 1975.
       (begin)

Many people _____ the project. Folklorists from Indiana University
     (run)

_____ to Gary, Indiana. The folklorists _____ students
 (go)   (be)

interested in old customs. They _____ to people from different
         (speak)

cultures. The folklorists _____ how families followed traditions. The
       (see)

Meléndez family still _____ Puerto Rican foods. Mrs. Meléndez
      (eat)

_____ the group traditional folk tales. Philip _____
 (tell)   (write)

down what she said. I _____ glad that I attended.
     (be)

Check your answers on page 222.

Forming the Future Tense

The **future tense** shows that something will happen at a later date. The future tense of all verbs is formed with the helping verb *will* and a main verb.

▶ I <u>will be</u> at home tonight.

▶ He <u>will come</u> to my house next week.

▶ Soon, we <u>will have</u> the arrangements ready.

Time clues that can help you recognize the future tense include *tomorrow, next year,* and *a day from now.*

PART A

In the blank, write the future tense of the verb in parentheses.

▶ Tomorrow, the Gonzales family ___*will leave*___ for Mexico.
(leave)

1. They _____ in Brownsville on the way.
   (stop)

2. Maria and Carlo _____ them there.
   (join)

3. Next week, the family _____ in Mexico City.
   (be)

4. Soon, little Linda _____ her grandmother.
   (meet)

5. They all _____ many interesting things.
   (do)

6. In two weeks, the family _____ home.
   (return)

PART B

Write a sentence for each verb in parentheses. In each sentence, use one of the time clues listed at the top of this page.

▶ (go)   *Tomorrow, I will go shopping.*

1. (win)   _____

2. (learn)   _____

3. (make)   _____

Check your answers on page 222.

Forming the Continuous Tenses

The **continuous tenses** are used to show actions in progress. The **present continuous tense** shows that something is happening at the moment of speaking or is in progress at the present time. It is formed by using *am, is,* or *are* as a helping verb with a main verb ending in *ing*.

▶ What <u>are</u> you <u>doing</u>? I <u>am</u> <u>watching</u> TV.

▶ People <u>are</u> <u>trying</u> to protect the environment.

The **past continuous tense** is used to show that an action was in progress. It is formed by using *was* or *were* as a helping verb with a main verb ending in *ing*.

▶ What <u>were</u> you <u>doing</u> when I called? I <u>was sleeping</u>.

The **future continuous tense** shows that an action will be happening. It is formed by using *will be* as helping verbs with a main verb ending in *ing*.

▶ What <u>will</u> you <u>be doing</u> later? I <u>will be studying</u>.

PART A

Underline the correct form of the helping verb in parentheses.

▶ People (<u>are</u>, is) learning to take better care of themselves.

1. Not long ago, Americans (were, was) becoming couch potatoes.

2. The general health of the nation (were, was) growing worse.

3. These days, more people (are, is) taking care of themselves.

4. I (am, is) walking half an hour each day.

5. (Are, Is) you exercising?

6. Lynn (are, is) watching her children's diet.

PART B

Use the continuous verb form to answer each question.

▶ Where are you going? _I am going to the movies._

1. What are you doing? _____

2. What were you doing? _____

3. What will you be doing? _____

Check your answers on page 223.

Chapter 11 Review

This exercise is a review of the main rules you have studied in this chapter. Underline the correct verb form in parentheses.

▶ As a child, I (love, <u>loved</u>) westerns.

1. Back then, westerns (were, was) playing on every TV channel.

2. (Are, Is) you old enough to remember them?

3. The heroes (were, was) rugged and clever.

4. Today's detectives (look, looks) weak in comparison.

5. My father's favorite program (were, was) "Bonanza."

6. Little Joe often (run, ran) into a good fistfight.

7. In movies, Clint Eastwood (appear, appeared) as the "Man with No Name."

8. His spaghetti westerns (delights, delighted) all my friends.

9. In the late 1960s, westerns (fade, faded) from the scene.

10. But Eastwood and others (are, is) making westerns again.

11. A new generation (be, will be) watching them.

12. Maybe westerns soon (become, will become) popular again.

13. Dan and I still (rent, rents) videos of the old ones.

14. You probably (see, sees) our favorites on store shelves.

15. He also (catch, catches) reruns late at night.

16. Dan or his brother (tape, tapes) them if possible.

17. One network (show, shows) the old "Rawhide" series.

18. (Do, Does) you ever watch it?

19. Dan's brother (have, has) copies of the best ones.

20. Will you (watch, watched) some with us tonight?

Check your answers on page 223.

CHAPTER 12 | MORE ABOUT VERBS

Using the Present Perfect

An action in the **present perfect tense** begins in the past and continues in the present.

▶ Mr. Hinojosa <u>has opened</u> his shop at 9:00 A.M. for years.

The present perfect also can show that something happened one or more times at an unspecified time in the past.

▶ Mr. Hinojosa and his wife <u>have visited</u> Canada.

To form the present perfect of a regular verb, use the appropriate form of the helping verb *have* and the past participle of the verb. Form the past participle of regular verbs by adding *d* or *ed* to the main verb. Don't confuse the present perfect with the past tense. Look for time clues that tell which tense to use.

▶ Last fall, we <u>moved</u>. For the past year, we <u>have enjoyed</u> city life.

Moved happened at a specific time in the past. *Have enjoyed* began in the past and continues in the present.

In the blank, write the correct tense of the verb in parentheses.

▶ Mrs. Maizel's husband _____*died*_____ ten years ago.
(die)

▶ Mrs. Maizel ___*has lived*___ alone since his death.
(live)

1. Until recently, her house _____ clean and tidy.
(look)

2. But for the past several months, it _____ sloppy.
(look)

3. Visitors _____ a musty smell in the house.
(notice)

4. Several times, people _____ about her messy yard.
(complain)

5. Yesterday, our son _____ Mrs. Maizel his help.
(offer)

6. But the proud woman _____ .
(refuse)

Check your answers on page 223.

Using the Past Perfect

The **past perfect tense** shows that one past action took place before another. To form the past perfect of regular verbs, use the helping verb *had* and the past participle of the verb.

▶ The bus <u>had</u> <u>pulled</u> away by the time Abby reached the corner.

Don't confuse the past perfect with the present perfect and past tenses. Use the simple past to express an action that took place and no longer continues.

▶ In May of 1989, I <u>accepted</u> a full-time job at Toolworld.

Use the past perfect to show that one past action took place before another.

▶ Before then, I <u>had</u> <u>worked</u> part-time at the store.

Use the present perfect to show that a past action continues.

▶ Since then, I <u>have</u> <u>worked</u> my way up to assistant manager.

Underline the correct verb tense in parentheses.

▶ Yesterday, Al (<u>started</u>, has started) the day all wrong.

1. His alarm (failed, has failed) to go off.

2. Therefore, he (stayed, has stayed) in bed too long.

3. Al got up and (turned, had turned) on the coffeepot.

4. Soon, he realized that he (filled, had filled) the filter with oatmeal.

5. The toast (has burned, had burned) before Al noticed.

6. Al didn't eat because he (wasted, had wasted) so much time.

7. As he began to shower, someone (phoned, had phoned).

8. By the time Al reached the phone, it (stopped, had stopped) ringing.

9. Poor Al said, "Everything (has worked, had worked) against me this morning!"

Check your answers on page 223.

Using Irregular Verbs I

Irregular verbs do not form the past participle with a *d* or *ed* ending. Here are the present, past, and past participle of some common irregular verbs.

Present	Past	Past Participle
am	was	been
be { is	was	been
are	were	been
become(s)	became	become
begin(s)	began	begun
blow(s)	blew	blown
break(s)	broke	broken
bring(s)	brought	brought

In the blanks, write the correct tense of the verb in parentheses—either present, past, or present or past perfect.

▶ (begin) Children _____*begin*_____ to walk at various ages. My son John _____*began*_____ to walk at eleven months. He had just _____*begun*_____ to walk when he broke his ankle.

1. (be) Here _____ my cats. They _____ under the bed a few minutes ago. They had _____ afraid to come out.

2. (become) Every day, people _____ American citizens. Keisha _____ a citizen last month. She has _____ used to living in the United States.

3. (break) My glasses _____ easily. I have _____ them many times. I _____ them again yesterday.

4. (blow) Every year, the wind _____ leaves into my yard. Last week, my next-door neighbor's leaves _____ into my yard. I wish the wind had _____ them somewhere else.

5. (bring) Mrs. Arlo always _____ a dessert. Last Sunday, she _____ a raisin pie. She has _____ a home-baked pie many times in the past.

Check your answers on page 223.

Using Irregular Verbs II

Here are the present, past, and past participle of some other common irregular verbs.

Present	Past	Past Participle
buy(s)	bought	bought
come(s)	came	come
do(es)	did	done
drink(s)	drank	drunk
eat(s)	ate	eaten
freeze(s)	froze	frozen

In the blanks, write the correct tense of the verb in parentheses—either present, past, or present or past perfect.

▶ (buy) I often ____buy____ things on sale. Once I ____bought____ an entire case of hot sauce. I realized I had ____bought____ enough for the whole neighborhood.

1. (come) He asked, "Why have you _____ to New York?" I replied, "I _____ to visit my sister. I _____ here every fall."

2. (do) Karen _____ her own taxes each April. Last year, she _____ mine too. She also has _____ my brother's taxes for three years in a row.

3. (drink) Mr. Estivez often _____ too much coffee. Yesterday, we _____ coffee in our favorite café. Before I could finish my first cup, he had _____ almost a potful.

4. (eat) My dog _____ too much. Last week, he _____ almost an entire loaf of bread. He has _____ bread before.

5. (freeze) The local pond _____ every winter. This morning, kids started skating on it as soon as the water had _____. Last winter, the pond _____ in early November.

Check your answers on page 223.

Using Irregular Verbs III

Here are the present, past, and past participle of some other common irregular verbs.

Present	Past	Past Participle
give(s)	gave	given
go(es)	went	gone
grow(s)	grew	grown
have (has)	had	had
know(s)	knew	known
run(s)	ran	run
see(s)	saw	seen

In the blanks, write the correct tense of the verb in parentheses—either present, past, or present or past perfect.

▶ (give) Ms. Fu ___*gives*___ karate lessons on Tuesdays. She

___*gave*___ me my first lesson several months ago. Her son had

___*given*___ the lessons until last March.

1. (go) We _____ to the movies once a week. We have _____

for several years. Last night, we _____ to the Rialto.

2. (grow) Every summer, Mrs. Ray _____ tomatoes. Over the years,

she has _____ hundreds. Last year, she _____ dozens.

3. (have) Our public library _____ an annual book sale. Many times,

I have _____ a hand in organizing the event. Last year, we

_____ more than $1,000 in sales.

4. (know) Angel always _____ how to solve math problems.

Last week, she even _____ the answer to a trick question. Has she

always _____ how to do math this well?

5. (run) James _____ a mile a day. I have _____ with him

many times. Last year, he _____ a marathon race and won.

6. (see) We _____ our cousins on holidays. I _____ them

last Easter. Have you _____ your cousins?

Check your answers on page 223.

Using Irregular Verbs IV

Here are the present, past, and past participle of some other common irregular verbs.

Present	Past	Past Participle
sing(s)	sang	sung
speak(s)	spoke	spoken
steal(s)	stole	stolen
take(s)	took	taken
tell(s)	told	told
write(s)	wrote	written

In the blanks, write the correct tense of the verb in parentheses—either present, past, or present or past perfect.

▶ (sing) Every Sunday, Anzia ___*sings*___ in the choir. Last Christmas, she ___*sang*___ her first solo. Since then, she has ___*sung*___ three solos.

1. (speak) Ms. Molinaro _____ excellent English. Until she moved to the United States, she had _____ only Spanish. She first _____ English five years ago.

2. (steal) I _____ time from work to be with my kids. Yesterday, I _____ an hour for a picnic. I wish that I could have _____ more time.

3. (take) Please _____ the trash out tonight. Your sister_____ it out last time. You haven't _____ it out for several days.

4. (tell) Juan sometimes _____ jokes. Last night he _____ a good one. I was the one who had _____ it to him.

5. (write) Vonda McIntyre_____ science fiction novels. She has _____ Star Trek novels. In 1986, she_____ my favorite, *Enterprise: the First Adventure.*

Check your answers on page 223.

Forming the Passive Voice

The **passive voice** is used to show that a subject is acted on. The passive voice is made up of a form of *be* and a verb in the past participle.

Passive: <u>Soap operas</u> <u>are watched</u> by many people.
Active: Many <u>people</u> <u>watch</u> soap operas.

The first sentence is passive because the subject, *soap operas*, receives the action (*watch*). The second sentence is active because the subject, *people*, does the action (*watch*). When using the passive voice, make sure the verb is in the past participle form.

▶ Soap operas are (saw, <u>seen</u>) all over the nation.

Underline and correct the participle error in each sentence.

▶ Writers of soap operas are <u>encourage</u> to create wild plots. *encouraged*

1. Characters are kidnap for strange reasons.

2. Natalie of "All My Children" was imprison by her sister.

3. On "Loving," Trisha's baby was stole by a boyfriend.

4. Often, the victims are rescue by mysterious strangers.

5. "One Life to Live" is praise for its up-to-date story lines.

6. Tom and Olivia were saw as examples of interracial romance.

7. Their relationship was complicate by their pasts.

8. Soap opera characters are face with more problems in six months than most people encounter in a lifetime.

9. Viewers object when their favorite program is interrupt by a news bulletin.

10. My favorite soap was took off the air many years ago.

Check your answers on page 223.

Using Participles

The past participle form of a verb may be used as an adjective. **Participles** describe an action that has been performed on a noun or pronoun.

▶ I ate a <u>poached</u> egg. (The egg has been poached.)

Do not omit *d* or *ed* endings from regular verbs used as participles. Be sure to use the correct form of irregular verbs.

▶ They sell (prewash, <u>prewashed</u>) jeans.

▶ The police returned the (stole, <u>stolen</u>) car to its owner.

PART A

Turn the underlined phrase into a one-word participle.

▶ His heart <u>has been broken</u>. He has a ___broken___ heart.

1. Their assets <u>have been frozen</u>. They are _____ assets.

2. The home <u>has been remodeled</u>. It is a _____ home.

3. The edition <u>has been revised</u>. It is a _____ edition.

4. The skirt <u>has been pleated</u>. It is a _____ skirt.

5. That book <u>has been banned</u>. It is a _____ book.

PART B

Underline and correct the participle error in each sentence.

▶ They served <u>glaze</u> *glazed* ham as the main course of the dinner.

Tom brought a huge bowl of mash potatoes. Helene made her famous pickle beets. Gordon prepared a delicious casserole of bake sweet potatoes, apples, and sausage. I brought butter carrots and peas. For dessert, Lena brought strawberry shortcake with whip cream. Burton brought poach pears in a delicious sauce.

Check your answers on page 224.

Using Fixed-Form Helpers

The **fixed-form helping verbs** are *can, could, may, might, shall, should, will,* and *must.* These helping verbs are unusual because their form never changes. Unlike the helping verbs *have* and *be*, fixed form helpers do not change form to agree with the subject.

▶ I <u>have</u> gone. He <u>has</u> gone.

▶ I <u>can</u> go. He <u>can</u> go.

Also unlike the helping verbs *have* and *be*, fixed-form helpers are not followed by the past participle form of the verb. Notice that the main verb takes no ending.

PART A

Underline the correct verb form in parentheses.

▶ Computer skills (<u>can help</u>, can helped) you in your job.

1. Years ago, only experts (could use, could used) computers.

2. Today, the average worker (must have, must has) basic computer skills.

3. Ted (may attend, may attended) classes given by his company.

4. He (should take, should takes) advantage of the offer.

5. You (can learn, can learned) about computers too.

6. I (might try, might tried) it myself.

7. Another class (will start, will starts) soon.

8. I (shall go, shall went) if I have time.

PART B

Write a sentence for each helping verb in parentheses.

▶ (might) ___I might buy a car._____

1. (can) _____

2. (may) _____

3. (should) _____

Check your answers on page 224.

Chapter 12 Review

This exercise is a review of the main rules you have studied in this chapter. Underline the correct verb form in parentheses.

► Most people (<u>have used</u>, had used) a dictionary.

1. You (<u>can look</u>, can looked) up word meanings in dictionaries.

2. Over the years, publishers (have issued, had issued) dictionaries of slang, foreign languages, and science.

3. A medical dictionary (might describe, might describes) a disease.

4. Have you (knew, known) anyone who worked on a dictionary?

5. The first English dictionary (was wrote, was written) in 1604 by Robert Cawdrey.

6. His work (was limit, was limited) to 3,000 "hard" words.

7. More than a century later, Samuel Johnson (created, has created) a dictionary of ordinary English words.

8. By the time he was finished, Johnson (has defined, had defined) 40,000 words.

9. In 1840, Noah Webster published his (revise, revised) edition of 70,000 definitions of American English.

10. Editions of Webster's book (have become, has become) standard references in public schools.

11. Students use the dictionaries to correct (misspell, misspelled) words.

12. Until the computer was invented, the organization of a dictionary (has been, had been) the task of many individuals.

13. Now, much of the boring work (is did, is done) by computer.

Check your answers on page 224.

CHAPTER 13 | ADJECTIVES AND ADVERBS

Identifying Adjectives

An **adjective** describes a noun or a pronoun by telling what kind, which one, or how many.

What kind: I collect <u>stoneware</u> mugs.
Which one: Bring me the <u>other</u> mug.
How many: I now have more than <u>fifty</u> mugs.

Underline the adjective that describes the boldface noun.

▶ For centuries, <u>folk</u> **potteries** have existed in South Korea.

1. Today, this **tradition** is dying out.

2. Few **potters** now make traditional wares.

3. These people live in remote **areas** of the country.

4. The pottery in Bu Chang Myun lies far off the main **road**.

5. Its three kilns fire earthenware in seven **days**.

6. Firing is the heating of the clay **pots**.

7. The kilns are huge **ovens** fueled by wood.

8. A smaller **pottery** is owned by Kim Hyun-Schick.

9. He has found a good **way** to shorten the firing time.

10. A shorter **firing** means lower costs.

11. These potteries produce roof **tiles**.

12. They also make storage **jars** for pickled vegetables.

13. Korean **potters** may also work with delicate porcelain.

14. They are re-creating ancient **glazes**.

15. These **people** are proud of their work.

Check your answers on page 224.

Finding Adjectives in Sentences

Adjectives often come directly before the nouns they describe.

▶ At times, people need <u>legal</u> <u>advice</u>.

However, adjectives can also come after the nouns they describe. Adjectives that come after nouns usually follow forms of the verb *be* or other verbs that do not show action.

▶ His <u>plan</u> is <u>legal</u>.

Underline the adjective that describes the boldface noun or pronoun. In the blank, write *A* if the adjective comes after the noun or pronoun or *B* if it comes before.

A   ▶ **Laws** are necessary.

B   ▶ Officials try to write good **laws**.

_____ **1. Laws** usually seem sensible.

_____ **2.** They help protect innocent **people**.

_____ **3.** But sometimes **laws** seem weird.

_____ **4.** Dick Hyman has written a book about strange **laws**.

_____ **5.** Some have reasonable **explanations**.

_____ **6.** A law in Ouray, Colorado, provides one **example**.

_____ **7. It** is illegal to hunt elk on Ouray's Main Street.

_____ **8.** You might think **this** is funny.

_____ **9.** But in mountain **towns**, elk can get in the street.

_____ **10.** A law in Massachusetts provides another **example**.

_____ **11.** Debt **collectors** can't wear costumes on the job.

_____ **12.** The law prevents collectors from pretending to be police **officers**.

_____ **13.** My town has **laws** that seem pointless.

_____ **14.** Are there unusual **laws** in your town?

Check your answers on page 224.

Identifying Adverbs

An **adverb** describes a verb, adjective, or other adverb. Adverbs tell how, how much, when, or where.

How:	Cara walked <u>quickly</u> down the street.
How much:	She was <u>very</u> upset.
When:	Cara <u>suddenly</u> felt ill.
Where:	She didn't have <u>anywhere</u> to go.

Many adverbs end in *ly*. A few common adverbs that do not are *almost, never, not, quite, very,* and *too*. Often an adverb comes directly after the word it describes. However, adverbs can appear anywhere in a sentence.

▶ <u>Here</u> is our new house.

▶ We are <u>slowly</u> repairing it.

▶ We wish we could move in <u>immediately</u>.

PART A
Match each adverb with the question it answers.

___*d*___ ▶ here   **(a)** How?

_____ **1.** immediately   **(b)** How much?

_____ **2.** carefully   **(c)** When?

_____ **3.** quite   **(d)** Where?

PART B
Underline the adverb that describes the boldface word or words. The question in parentheses will help you find the adverb.

▶ Stress <u>sometimes</u> **bothers** people. (When?)

1. Stress can affect people **living** anywhere. (Where?)

2. At times, a person **may react** negatively. (How?)

3. Some people immediately **panic**. (When?)

4. But some people **handle** stress well. (How?)

5. For them, stress is very **positive**. (How much?)

Check your answers on page 224.

Forming Adjectives and Adverbs

If you want to describe a noun or a pronoun, use an adjective. If you want to describe a verb, adjective, or adverb, use an adverb. In many cases, you can turn an adjective into an adverb by adding an *ly* ending to the adjective.

Adjective describing noun: The <u>fierce</u> wind blew.
Adverb describing verb: The wind blew <u>fiercely</u>.

In the blank, write the correct form—adjective or adverb—of the word in parentheses. You will use each word twice.

▶ (slow)   Nigel is a ___*slow*___ driver.

He ___*slowly*___ pulled up to the curb.

1. (careful)   Rusty is a _____ carpenter.

He measures _____ before sawing boards.

2. (soft)   My new carpet feels very _____ .

My mother walked _____ across the floor.

3. (strong)   Alan _____ opposed the helmet law.

Alan has _____ opinions about politics.

4. (correct)   The teacher checked for _____ answers.

Dave answered all the questions _____ .

5. (pleasant) Mary is a _____ woman.

She always smiles _____ at people.

6. (heavy)   Emil sighed _____ after lifting the carton.

The carton was very _____ .

7. (usual)   I will meet Sharon at the _____ place.

We _____ meet at 6:30 P.M.

8. (gentle)   Babies require a _____ touch.

The mother _____ picked up her baby.

Check your answers on page 225.

Choosing Adjectives or Adverbs

Do not confuse the adjective and adverb forms of a word. In the sentence below, the adverb *really* describes the adjective *good*.

▶ *The Miracle Worker* is a (real, <u>really</u>) good movie.

In the next example, the adjective *real* describes the noun *treat*.

▶ Watching it is a (<u>real</u>, really) treat.

PART A
Underline the correct form—adjective or adverb—in parentheses.

▶ A (<u>serious</u>, seriously) childhood illness made Helen Keller a deaf-mute.

1. The only sounds she made were (loud, loudly) noises.

2. She was also (complete, completely) blind.

3. Helen's parents hired a (hopeful, hopefully) young teacher.

4. Anne Sullivan worked (patient, patiently) with the child.

5. Helen (slow, slowly) learned to read and write in Braille.

6. By age sixteen, Helen could speak (clear, clearly) enough to go to school.

7. As an adult, Keller was (active, actively) in organizations for the blind.

8. Her accomplishments were (true, truly) impressive.

PART B
Underline and correct the adjective or adverb error in each sentence.

▶ Moshe thinks he sings <u>beautiful</u>. beautifully

Actually, his singing is awfully. Everyone leaves the room quick when Moshe starts to sing. If he sang quietly, it wouldn't be so badly. But his voice is loudly enough to wake the dead!

Check your answers on page 225.

Making Comparisons with Adjectives

These guidelines will help you use adjectives in **comparisons**.

To compare two people or things, add an *er* ending to short adjectives (of one or two syllables). Notice that with some two-syllable adjectives the word *more* or *less* takes the place of the *er* ending.

▶ Jack may be <u>older</u> than I am, but I am <u>more</u> <u>clever</u>.

Long adjectives (of three or more syllables) do not take an *er* ending when used to compare two people or things. The word *more* or *less* is used with these adjectives.

▶ My household accounts are <u>more</u> <u>accurate</u> than his.

To make a comparison among three or more people or things, add an *est* ending to short adjectives. Notice that a few two-syllable adjectives use *most* or *least* instead.

▶ I am the <u>smartest</u>, but Jack is the <u>most</u> <u>skilled</u>.

Long adjectives that compare three or more people or things do not end in *est*. Use *most* or *least* with these adjectives.

▶ Of all the kids, Jack is the <u>least</u> rebellious.

Never use *more, less, most,* or *least* with an adjective ending in *er* or *est*.

▶ He is the (most tidiest, <u>tidiest</u>) man I know.

Underline the correct form of the adjective in parentheses.

▶ Rivermen were our (more colorful, <u>most colorful</u>) heroes.

1. They took pride in being (tougher, toughest) than most.

2. They were the (less modest, least modest) of all heroes.

3. Mike Fink was the (more famous, most famous) riverman.

4. He bragged that he was the (strongest, most strongest).

5. He also claimed to be (faster, more faster) than other men.

6. Davy Crockett was said to be (less skilled, least skilled) with a rifle than Fink.

Check your answers on page 225.

Using Irregular Adjectives

Irregular adjectives change form when they are used in comparisons. The two most common irregulars are *good* and *bad*.

No Comparison	Comparing Two	Comparing Three or More
good	better	best
bad	worse	worst

▶ Woody was a <u>better</u> singer than Arlo.

▶ Martin is the <u>worst</u> singer I have ever heard.

Do not use *more* or *most* with irregular adjectives. Do not add *er* or *est* endings.

▶ His cold is (worser, <u>worse</u>) today than it was yesterday.

▶ The medicine will make him feel (<u>better</u>, more better).

PART A

In the blank, write the correct form of the word in parentheses.

▶ This year's company picnic was the __**best**__ ever.
  (good)

1. The _____ of all was last year's, when it stormed.
  (bad)

2. Mahmud made the _____ potato salad I've ever tasted.
  (good)

3. I must admit that it was even _____ than my own.
  (good)

4. I was the _____ of all the volleyball players.
  (bad)

5. I was even _____ than Myra, who had a sprained wrist.
  (bad)

PART B

Underline and correct the adjective error in each sentence.

▶   "M*A*S*H" was one of the <u>most best</u> TV shows I've ever seen.
  best

I think that the TV show was even more better than the movie. The most worstest

TV show was "My Mother the Car." It actually was worser than "Three's Company."

Check your answers on page 225.

Making Comparisons with Adverbs

These guidelines will help you use adverbs in comparisons.

When comparing two people or things, use the words *more* or *less* with adverbs that end in *ly*. Use *most* or *least* with these adverbs when comparing three or more people or things.

▶ Sally ran <u>more quickly</u> than Randall. In fact, Sally ran the <u>most quickly</u> of all the runners.

To make comparisons with adverbs that do not end in *ly*, add an *er* ending (when comparing two people or things) or an *est* ending (when comparing three or more people or things).

▶ Alma types <u>faster</u> than I, but Mal types <u>fastest</u> of all.

The adverb *well* is irregular. When comparing two people or things, use *better*. When comparing three or more, use *best*.

▶ Ruth did <u>well</u>. Alfie did <u>better</u>. Ron did the <u>best</u>.

Underline the correct form of the adverb in parentheses.

▶ Some people age (<u>more gracefully</u>, gracefuller) than others.

1. At 105 years of age, Pete Lavoy plays (harder, more hard) than many people half his age.

2. Does Lavoy age (less rapid, less rapidly) than most of us?

3. Or does he just live life (more fully, fuller)?

4. He gets around (more well, better) than you can imagine.

5. Lavoy told reporters that of his many interests, he is still (more actively, most actively) involved in farming.

6. Lavoy also said he exercises (more frequently, frequentlier) than many of his younger neighbors.

7. Lavoy claims he can pick corn (quicker, more quickly) than any other farmer in the area.

Check your answers on page 225.

Revising Double Negatives

Some words are negative in meaning. Common negatives are *no, not, never, nothing, nobody, no one, none, hardly,* and *scarcely*. Do not use one of these negatives in combination with another negative. This error is known as a **double negative**.

> **Incorrect**: The Abdullah family did <u>not</u> ask for <u>no</u> help.
> **Correct**: The Abdullah family did <u>not</u> ask for <u>any</u> help.

The adverb *not* can combine with helping verbs to make contractions. Don't use *ain't* in place of *isn't, aren't, haven't,* or *don't*.

> **Incorrect:** Mrs. Abdullah <u>ain't</u> home.
> **Correct:** Mrs. Abdullah <u>isn't</u> home.

Circle the letter of the correctly worded sentence in each pair.

▶ **(a)** I couldn't afford to buy any milk.
  (b) I couldn't afford to buy no milk.

1. **(a)** We have scarcely enough money to pay the rent.
   (b) We haven't scarcely enough money to pay the rent.

2. **(a)** I don't know anything about budgeting money.
   (b) I don't know nothing about budgeting money.

3. **(a)** No one has never offered us any help.
   (b) No one has ever offered us any help.

4. **(a)** Anyway, we wouldn't accept no charity.
   (b) Anyway, we wouldn't accept any charity.

5. **(a)** But we can't pay none of these bills.
   (b) But we can't pay any of these bills.

6. **(a)** I haven't ever felt so unhappy.
   (b) I ain't ever felt so unhappy.

7. **(a)** I don't hardly know what to do.
   (b) I hardly know what to do.

Check your answers on page 225.

Chapter 13 Review

This exercise is a review of the main rules you have studied in this chapter. Underline the correct adjective or adverb form in parentheses.

▶ Hurricanes are (<u>natural</u>, naturally) disasters.

1. Hurricanes start as (whirling, whirlingly) masses of air.

2. These storms are the (more, most) destructive on earth.

3. Hurricane Andrew was one of the (worse, worst) storms that ever hit the United States.

4. Of the two states hit, Louisiana was (less, least) damaged.

5. In an (unbelievable, unbelievably) short time, thousands of people in Florida had lost their homes.

6. Many families found they had (almost, hardly) nothing left.

7. (Entire, Entirely) towns in Florida were ruined.

8. People didn't have (no, any) electricity or water.

9. Relief efforts were organized (immediate, immediately).

10. The Red Cross was (bestest, best) prepared to help.

11. Volunteers worked (tireless, tirelessly) to help.

12. The amount of relief money donated by private citizens was (impressive, impressively).

13. The government sent aid, but (more slowly, slowlier) than some had hoped.

14. The army set up (large, largely) tent cities.

15. Thousands had no (more better, better) place to live.

16. Survival became (more, most) important than anything else.

17. Recovery from such a disaster happens (slow, slowly).

18. Victims (ain't, aren't) ever going to forget the hurricane.

Check your answers on page 225.

CHAPTER 14 | SENTENCES AND PUNCTUATION

Using End Marks

A sentence should be followed by an **end mark**—a period, question mark, or exclamation point.

Put a period at the end of a **statement**—a sentence that gives information.
▶ The elevator is over there.

Put a question mark at the end of a **question**—a sentence that asks something.
▶ Where are you going?

Put an exclamation point at the end of an **exclamation**—a sentence that shows strong feeling.
▶ We won!

Put a period at the end of a **command**—a sentence that tells someone to do something. If the command shows strong feeling, use an exclamation point.
▶ Wait for me here.
▶ Call the fire department!

In the blank, write the correct end mark.

▶ The elevator door is stuck.

1. We're trapped__

2. Please try to stay calm__

3. Now, press the emergency button__

4. The door is opening__

5. Do you know how the modern elevator was developed__

6. In 1852, Elisha Otis added a safety device to hoists__

7. His invention stopped hoists from falling suddenly__

8. Can you imagine tall buildings without elevators__

Check your answers on page 225.

Understanding Simple Sentences

A **simple sentence** consists of one independent clause. An **independent clause** has a subject and a predicate and expresses a complete thought. The **subject** is the person, place, or thing the clause is about. The **predicate** tells what the subject does or is. The predicate always contains a verb or verbs.

> ▶ Frederick Douglass was a leader of the antislavery movement.
>
> **Subject:** Frederick Douglass
> **Predicate:** was a leader of the antislavery movement.
> **Verb:** was

Draw a line between the subject and predicate.

▶ Frederick Douglass / was the son of a black slave woman.

1. Most slave owners didn't want slaves to read or write.

2. Mrs. Auld broke the law in Maryland.

3. This slave owner taught young Douglass how to read.

4. Mr. Auld beat Douglass for learning.

5. Douglass escaped slavery in 1838.

6. He began to speak out against slavery.

7. People were inspired by Douglass's words.

8. Douglass wrote a book about his life.

9. The book is called *Life and Times of Frederick Douglass.*

10. You should read it.

11. Douglass held a government post later in his life.

12. He served as a U.S. minister and consul general to Haiti from 1889 to 1891.

Check your answers on page 225.

Understanding Compound Sentences I

A **compound sentence** is made up of two simple sentences (independent clauses) joined by a **coordinating conjunction**—*and, but, yet, so, nor, or,* or *for.* Put a comma before the coordinating conjunction in a compound sentence.

Simple Sentence:	Julio is studying.
Simple Sentence:	Toshiro is helping.
Compound Sentence:	Julio is studying, <u>and</u> Toshiro is helping.

Do not put a comma before a coordinating conjunction that is not joining independent clauses.

▶ Julio feels frustrated <u>and</u> is tired of reading.

Underline the coordinating conjunction. Add a comma before the conjunction when needed.

▶ Amelia Bloomer was a feminist writer, <u>but</u> she is better remembered for her unusual outfits.

▶ Bloomer didn't mean to set a fashion <u>nor</u> to become famous.

1. She supported women's rights and spoke out against slavery.

2. Bloomer disliked clumsy hoopskirts so she wore loose trousers under a short skirt.

3. Her clothes attracted a lot of attention for women didn't usually wear trousers in the mid-1800s.

4. Bloomer thought her clothing was practical but many people were shocked.

5. People stared rudely or laughed at her "bloomers."

6. The trouser outfit didn't catch on yet the term *bloomers* is still remembered.

Check your answers on page 226.

Understanding Compound Sentences II

There is a second way to form compound sentences. Join the two simple sentences (independent clauses) with a semicolon, a conjunctive adverb, and a comma.

> **Simple Sentence:** I felt ill.
> **Simple Sentence:** I left early.
> **Compound Sentence:** I felt ill; therefore, I left early.

Here are some common **conjunctive adverbs,** grouped by the coordinating conjunction they most closely resemble in meaning.

and	**so**	**but**	**or**
moreover	therefore	on the other hand	otherwise
furthermore	as a result	however	
in addition	thus		

Join each pair of sentences with a semicolon, an appropriate conjunctive adverb, and a comma.

▶ You must study ; _otherwise,_ you will not pass the test.

1. George was bored with his job _____ he wanted a position with higher pay.

2. He needed to learn new skills _____ he decided to go back to school.

3. The classes were tough _____ he managed to pass them.

4. The school told George about job openings _____ it taught him how to answer interviewers' questions.

5. George's new job in marketing is fun _____ the salary and the benefits are good.

6. Sometimes, people have to learn new skills _____ they may get stuck in dead-end jobs.

Check your answers on page 226.

Fixing Run-Ons and Comma Splices

Two common sentence errors are run-ons and comma splices.

A **run-on sentence** occurs when two sentences are joined without a conjunction or proper punctuation.

▶ The electrician is late he will try to hurry.

A **comma splice** occurs when two sentences are joined by a comma but no conjunction.

▶ The electrician is late, he will try to hurry.

Here are three ways to fix run-ons and comma splices.

1. Separate the two sentences with a period.
    ▶ The electrician is late. He will try to hurry.

2. Form a compound sentence with a coordinating conjunction (and, but, yet, so, nor, or, for).
    ▶ The electrician is late, but he will try to hurry.

3. Form a compound sentence with a conjunctive adverb (A list of these conjuctions is on page 182.)
    ▶ The electrician is late; however, he will try to hurry.

Correct the six comma splices and four run-on sentences by using the methods described above. Use each method at least once.

▶ Manoli bought a used TV. the owner said it still worked.

On the first day, the set worked fine the picture disappeared the next day. Manoli thought the TV could be fixed, a repair shop was just down the street. The clerk said the set was old they couldn't fix it. Manoli was disappointed, he didn't want to throw out the TV. The set wasn't really old, why couldn't it be repaired?

The yellow pages had a list of repair shops others were advertised in the newspapers. Manoli called several, his wife called the rest. A man at a shop said he could help, Manoli took the TV in. The repair took only a few minutes a tiny part had been broken. Manoli was pleased, his TV worked for several years after that.

Check your answers on page 226.

Understanding Complex Sentences I

A **complex sentence** is made up of one independent clause and one or more dependent clauses. A **dependent clause** has a subject and a predicate, but it cannot stand alone as a sentence because it is not a complete thought. Dependent clauses start with **subordinating conjunctions**.

Common Subordinating Conjunctions		
after	before	until
although	if	when
as	since	where
because	though	while

Put a comma after a dependent clause that begins a sentence.

▶ <u>When opportunity knocks</u>, you should open the door.

When a dependent clause follows an independent clause, no comma is used to separate the two.

▶ You should open the door <u>when opportunity knocks</u>.

Underline the dependent clause. If the dependent clause begins the sentence, add a comma after the clause.

▶ <u>When Tony lost his job,</u> he started to worry about money.

▶ Tony has been looking for work <u>since the factory closed</u>.

1. Jobs have been hard to find because no one is hiring.

2. Until he finds employment Tony will have to spend less.

3. Tony found a page of coupons while he was reading the paper.

4. Tony made a shopping list before he went to the store.

5. After he made his list he found coupons for some items.

6. Though each coupon gave only cents off the savings added up.

7. Tony will save money if he continues to use coupons.

8. You, too, should use coupons when you shop.

Check your answers on page 226.

Understanding Complex Sentences II

A **relative clause** is a special kind of dependent clause. It begins with a relative pronoun—*who, which,* or *that*. Relative clauses are punctuated differently from other dependent clauses. **Nonessential** relative clauses are set off with commas. **Essential** relative clauses are not set off.

Relative clauses that begin with *which* are nonessential.

▶   *Awakenings*, which is my favorite movie, is on video.

▶   It is about encephalitis, which is a brain disease.

Relative clauses that begin with *that* are essential.

▶   I hope that you get a chance to see the movie.

Relative clauses that begin with *who* may be essential or nonessential. An essential clause identifies the noun or pronoun it describes. A nonessential clause does not.

▶   I like the actors who star in the film.

The clause is needed to identify which actors are liked.

▶   I like Robin Williams, who stars in the film.

The clause is not needed to identify the noun it describes—Robin Williams. Therefore, the clause is nonessential.

Underline each relative clause. Punctuate nonessential clauses.

▶ Unicorns are horned horses that exist only in fairy tales.

▶ Children often believe in unicorns, which are said to have magical powers.

1. Bigfoot is a legendary beast that some adults believe in.

2. Reports of Bigfoot sightings which are badly documented have been studied by scientists.

3. People who believe in Bigfoot try to prove its existence.

4. John Napier who worked for the Smithsonian Institution wrote a book about the creature.

5. Napier believes in the yeti which is similar to Bigfoot.

Check your answers on page 226.

Correcting Sentence Fragments I

A **sentence fragment** is an incomplete sentence capitalized and punctuated as if it were complete. One common type of sentence fragment occurs when a writer capitalizes and puts a period after a dependent clause.

▶ Luis was worried. <u>Because he lost his job.</u>

▶ I wrote to Sharon Naus. <u>Who is our insurance agent.</u>

Correct fragments by combining them with independent clauses.

▶ Luis was worried <u>because he lost his job.</u>

▶ I wrote to Sharon Naus, <u>who is our insurance agent.</u>

Underline the sentence fragments. Then rewrite the paragraph so that there are no fragments. Be sure to punctuate correctly.

▶ I worry about the cost of health care. Which keeps rising.

<u>I worry about the cost of health care, which keeps rising.</u>

The problem lies in the growing cost of insurance premiums. Which are too expensive for many people. Many children don't get proper medical care. Because parents can't afford it. Although many families still have medical insurance. They may not be able to pay for it in the future. Many people may suffer. If something is not done soon. This problem has been recognized by many doctors, including C. Everett Koop. Who used to be the surgeon general.

_____

_____

_____

_____

_____

_____

Check your answers on page 226.

Correcting Sentence Fragments II

Sentence fragments also occur when writers capitalize and punctuate phrases as if they were complete sentences. A **phrase** is a group of words that may include a subject or a predicate but not both. As a result, a phrase does not state a complete thought and cannot stand alone as a complete sentence. To correct fragments that are phrases, figure out what is missing—a subject or a predicate or both. Then add the missing part or combine the phrase with a complete sentence.

Fragment:	The president of the company. (no predicate)
Sentence:	The president of the company <u>called.</u>
Fragment:	Looked in the phone book. (no subject)
Sentence:	<u>Tim</u> looked in the phone book.

Underline the sentence fragments. Then rewrite the paragraph so that there are no fragments.

▶ Mrs. Ramirez went shopping. <u>At the local department store.</u>

<u>Mrs. Ramirez went shopping at the local department store.</u>

A helpful and friendly salesclerk. Showed Mrs. Ramirez several styles and colors. Mrs. Ramirez finally chose a green dress. In a few minutes, she trying it on. It was too big! Her new diet had worked. Mrs. Ramirez and the salesclerk both laughing. Then the two women looked. For a smaller-sized dress. Soon the pleased shopper. Selected and bought just the right dress.

_____

_____

_____

_____

_____

Check your answers on page 227.

Chapter 14 Review

This exercise is a review of the main rules you have studied in this chapter. Circle the letter of the correct sentence in each pair.

▶ **(a)** The Iroquois tribes united before America existed.
   (b) The Iroquois tribes united, before America existed.

1. **(a)** We read and talked about the tribes in school.
   (b) We read, and talked about the tribes in school.

2. **(a)** Five tribes created the system. That was called the League of Five Nations.
   (b) Five tribes created the system that was called the League of Five Nations.

3. **(a)** After the league was formed, the tribes stopped fighting each other.
   (b) After the league was formed the tribes stopped fighting each other.

4. **(a)** Their council, which consisted of fifty chiefs, handled business among the tribes.
   (b) Their council which consisted of fifty chiefs handled business among the tribes.

5. **(a)** The league had unwritten laws. Based on tribal needs.
   (b) The league had unwritten laws based on tribal needs.

6. **(a)** The tribes worked together each tribe governed itself.
   (b) The tribes worked together; however, each tribe governed itself.

7. **(a)** Women had power, for they appointed the chiefs.
   (b) Women had power, they appointed the chiefs.

8. **(a)** Did you know that Ben Franklin studied this system!
   (b) Did you know that Ben Franklin studied this system?

9. **(a)** Franklin, who helped plan the U.S. government, borrowed ideas from the Iroquois.
   (b) Franklin who helped plan the U.S. government borrowed ideas from the Iroquois.

Check your answers on page 227.

CHAPTER 15 | MORE ABOUT PUNCTUATION

Punctuating Series

A **series** consists of three or more similar items in a row. Put a comma after each item in a series except for the last one.

▶ **Right:** We are <u>ready</u>, <u>willing</u>, and <u>able</u> to join the fight.

▶ **Wrong:** We are <u>ready</u>, <u>willing</u>, and <u>able</u>, to join the fight.

If the word *and* or *or* is used between the items in a series, do not punctuate.

▶ **Right:** Selling takes hard work <u>and</u> patience <u>and</u> a little bit of luck.

▶ **Wrong:** Selling takes hard work<u>, and</u> patience<u>, and</u> a little bit of luck.

PART A

Add commas to each sentence where needed. If a sentence does not need commas, write OK in front of it. Proofread for series only.

▶ Darryl, June, and Frank have been good friends since grade school.

1. They plan to swim run play basketball and work part-time this summer.

2. Darryl will work at a restaurant on Tuesdays and Thursdays.

3. June and Frank will work Mondays Wednesdays and Fridays at Hank's.

4. The three friends love the Mets pizza and going to concerts.

5. They laugh and tell stories and have a great time whenever they get together.

PART B

Add commas to the paragraph where needed. Proofread for series only.

▶ Americans have changed the way they think about cars, energy, and the environment. Gas no longer seemed cheap or plentiful or something to take for granted after the oil crisis of the early 1970s. Some people began to commute in carpools take public transportation or bike to school or work. Others traded gas-guzzling cars for cheaper smaller more fuel-efficient models.

Check your answers on page 227.

Punctuating Dates and Addresses

Follow the examples below to punctuate dates correctly.

▶ My brother was born on <u>March 1, 1980</u>.

▶ I was born on<u> January 28, 1976,</u> in Maine.

▶ <u>January 1976</u> was a cold and snowy month.

To punctuate addresses correctly, follow these examples.

▶ The company is located in <u>Detroit, Michigan.</u>

▶ <u>Detroit, Michigan,</u> is the home of the Pistons.

▶ Send the letter to <u>Detroit, MI 48202</u>

Add commas to the letter where needed. Proofread for dates and addresses only.

27 Lloyd Street

Minneapolis MN 55401

July 25 19--

Charlene Ramirez, President

Ramirez Tire & Auto, Inc.

430 W. Stoney St.

Boston MA 02125

Dear Ms. Ramirez:

Your new year's offer of January 19-- promised $50 back on any two Ramirez tires purchased during this year. Enclosed are copies of sales receipts for tires purchased in your Hibbing Minnesota outlet store on October 17 19-- and on July 10 19--. Please send me the $50 rebate. Thank you.

Sincerely,

Ellis C. Turner

Ellis C. Turner

Check your answers on page 227.

Punctuating Appositives

An **appositive** is a word or words that give additional information about a noun or nouns. In the example below, the underlined appositive gives additional information about the noun *Soon-Bok* by explaining who she is.

▶ The meeting was led by Soon-Bok, the president of the school board.

Nonessential appositives are set off with commas.

▶ Whoopi Goldberg, an actress, is very talented.

The appositive is not needed to identify Whoopi Goldberg, the noun it describes.

Essential appositives are not set off with commas.

▶ Have you seen her movie *Sister Act*?

Whoopi Goldberg has starred in more than one movie. The appositive is needed to identify which movie the speaker means.

Add commas to each sentence where needed. If a sentence does not need commas, write OK in front of it. Proofread for appositives only.

▶ Whoopi Goldberg beat a drug problem with help from her first husband, a drug counselor.

1. She joined a theater group the San Diego Repertory Theatre and began to act in plays.

2. Have you read Alice Walker's novel *The Color Purple?*

3. In the film based on the novel, Goldberg played the role of Celie an abused woman.

4. Stephen Spielberg the director of *E.T.: The Extra Terrestrial* picked her for the role.

5. In *Ghost*, Goldberg played the role of Oda Mae Brown the character who helps Demi Moore and Patrick Swayze reunite.

6. This role won her an important award the Oscar for best supporting actress and led to parts in other movies.

7. She also has done stand-up comedy and appeared in the TV series "Star Trek: The Next Generation."

Check your answers on page 227.

Punctuating Direct Addresses

A **direct address** is the name or title of a person to whom a sentence is written or spoken. Set off direct addresses with commas.

▶ Larry, you're getting on my nerves.

▶ I swear, Judge Wopner, I didn't do it.

▶ Your husband is on line two, Ms. Trujillo.

PART A

Underline and punctuate the direct address in each sentence.

▶ I must say that your essay was simply terrific, James.

1. Veronika and Ernesto please take out the garbage.

2. I voted for you Senator Hillman in the last election.

3. Aunt Tereza I really appreciate the gift you sent me.

4. I care a great deal about you my friend.

PART B

Pick three of the names below or choose three of your own. For each name, write a sentence that contains a direct address. Put one of the direct addresses at the beginning of a sentence, one in the middle, and one at the end.

Run-D.M.C.	Fernando Valenzuela	Bart Simpson
Hillary Rodham Clinton	Arnold Schwarzenegger	Shaquille O'Neal
Monica Seles	Madonna	Michael Jordan
Prince Charles	Kramer	Garth Brooks

▶ How do you like polo, Prince Charles?

1. _____

2. _____

3. _____

Check your answers on page 227.

Punctuating Interrupters

An **interrupter** is a word or words that provide additional but nonessential information to a sentence. Interrupters momentarily interfere with the flow of a sentence.

▶ This is the best, though not the least expensive, way to prevent accidents.

▶ We have, so I'm told, the best safety record.

Often, interrupters are conjunctive adverbs (page 182) used to show transition rather than to link sentences.

▶ The work is hard. It is, on the other hand, rewarding.

▶ Our insurance is, in fact, the best available.

▶ I hope I never have to use it, however.

Punctuate the interrupter.

▶ Today, the average factory is relatively safe. That was not always the case however.

1. Many early factories were by today's standards terrible places.

2. Serious injuries were in fact common.

3. Certain practices most notably locking exits to prevent stealing led to disaster.

4. This method of theft control was dangerous to say the least.

5. Workers were unfortunately trapped when fire broke out.

6. By the late 1800s, working conditions though still bad began to improve.

7. Workers fed up with terrible conditions had begun to join unions and organize strikes.

8. Unions have of course played an important role in the history of the U.S. worker.

Check your answers on page 228.

Punctuating Introductory Items

Put a comma after a word, phrase, or clause that introduces a sentence.

Word:	<u>No,</u> you can't have ice cream before dinner.
	<u>However,</u> you can have some for dessert.
Phrase:	<u>Seeing his chance,</u> Mr. Hill ran out the door.
	<u>To my dismay,</u> I saw a parking ticket on my windshield.
	<u>Up ahead in the distance,</u> strange lights appeared.
Clause:	<u>Before you can run,</u> you have to learn to crawl.
	<u>If Maria gets back by 10:00 P.M.,</u> ask her to call me.

(See page 184 for more examples of introductory clauses.)

Do not put a comma after an introductory item if the rest of the sentence cannot stand on its own as a complete thought.

▶ <u>To know me</u> is to love me.

▶ <u>Running all over town</u> has made her tired.

Add a comma to each sentence where needed. If a sentence does not need a comma, write OK in front of it. Proofread for introductory items only.

▶ Because our club needs money, we're having a car wash this Saturday.

1. In case of rain the event will be held next Saturday.

2. However the weather should be fine this week.

3. If you have the time I hope you'll stop by.

4. Yes we'll also be washing vans and motorcycles.

5. At the end of the day we'll have a party at Sahana's house.

6. To make more money our club will hold a bake sale later this year.

7. Once we make enough money we'll be able to take a trip together.

8. Holding fund-raisers can be a lot of fun.

Check your answers on page 228.

Using the Colon

Put a colon after the salutation of a business letter.

▶ Dear Ms. Brown:

▶ Dear Sir:

Also put a colon after the phrase *the following* or *as follows* when it introduces a series or a list.

▶ Your job includes the following tasks: collecting rent, shoveling snow, and making any needed repairs.

▶ My goals for the summer are as follows:

   1. Lose weight

   2. Read five books

   3. Work out

Notice that a colon is used when the words preceding the series or list express a complete thought. If a complete thought does not precede the series or list, then a colon is not used.

Wrong:	Please bring: your I.D., your schedule, and a pen.
Right:	Please bring your I.D., your schedule, and a pen.
Right:	Please bring the following items: your I.D., your schedule, and a pen.

Add a colon in the space if needed. If no colon is needed, leave the space blank.

▶ Please send me the following CDs: "Mama Say Knock You Out," "Green," and "Exile on Main Street."

1. Dear Editor_

2. The people next door are_ loud, messy, and rude.

3. Gabriel's stats for the game were as follows_ 26 points, 10 assists, and 3 rebounds.

4. Dear Marquez Cleaners_

5. The following students should report for class on Tuesday_ Aaron, June, Cecily, and Raoul.

6. To Whom It May Concern_

Check your answers on page 228.

Using the Semicolon

Put a semicolon before a conjunctive adverb that joins two sentences. (See page 182 for more examples.)

▶ Terrence needs money to buy a new car. He has taken a second job.

▶ Terrence needs money to buy a new car; therefore, he has taken a second job.

Also use a semicolon to join two closely related sentences that are not separated by a conjunction.

▶ The score is tied. Let's not leave yet.

  The score is tied; let's not leave yet.

PART A

Join the two sentences with a semicolon, a conjunctive adverb, and a comma.

▶ He has his faults.
  I love him.
  (however) _He has his faults; however, I love him._

1. Football is a game of strength and speed.
   It takes brains and determination.
   (moreover) _____

2. Marticka, Ever, and Guadalupe were there.
   Marilu, Gina, and Ron couldn't make it.
   (however) _____

3. This tent had better be waterproof.
   We'll be in trouble if it rains.
   (otherwise) _____

PART B

Use a semicolon to separate the two sentences in each pair.

▶ L.L. Cool J has sold millions of albums; he's one of rap's best-known performers.

1. These shoes are too tight my feet are killing me.

2. Jenna read the book *Another Country* ask her about it.

3. Abandoned cars were everywhere litter filled the street.

4. Gardening is her favorite pastime she spends hours working in the dirt.

Check your answers on page 228.

Avoiding Common Punctuation Errors

Do not use a comma to separate a subject from its verb.

Wrong: The purpose of the assignment, is to help you develop your writing skills.

Right: The purpose of the assignment is to help you develop your writing skills.

Do not use a comma to separate a verb from its object.

Wrong: Paul owns, his own construction company.

Right: Paul owns his own construction company.

When setting off an appositive, interrupter, or other item in the middle of a sentence, be sure to use *both* commas.

Wrong: Sam's Groceries has if I'm not mistaken, the brand you want.

Right: Sam's Groceries has, if I'm not mistaken, the brand you want.

Wrong: My favorite holiday, Cinco de Mayo marks the beginning of spring.

Right: My favorite holiday, Cinco de Mayo, marks the beginning of spring.

If a sentence needs a comma, add one. If a sentence contains an unnecessary comma, cross out the comma. If a sentence is correctly punctuated, write OK in front of it.

▶ It's true that the United States is a nation of immigrants.

▶ My community, a very diverse place, has people from all over the world.

1. Mr. Wong, whom we met last weekend is from Taiwan.

2. Ben Harrison the man downstairs, is from England.

3. The family that owns this liquor store, is from India.

4. Kwame and Cynthia are from the West Indies.

5. Our neighborhood holds, a street fair each summer.

Check your answers on page 228.

Chapter 15 Review

This exercise is a review of the main rules you have studied in this chapter. Add commas, colons, or semicolons where needed.

7628 North Willard Street

Chicago IL 60648

April 8 19––

Yoder's Restaurant

5323 Wyman Way

Elmhurst IL 60126

Dear Mr. Yoder

I have enjoyed eating in your restaurant for many years. However I had a terrible experience there last night. My husband two friends and I had reservations for 8:00 P.M. and arrived right on time. Much to our annoyance the hostess Loretta Smith told us our table was not ready. Mr. Yoder we then waited 45 minutes. We wanted our friends to try your cornmeal rolls otherwise we would have left.

Finally we were seated. But our troubles were not over. During the course of the meal we suffered through the following problems warm salad cold soup and a waiter who dropped a drink in my husband's lap. Furthermore we learned that you no longer serve cornmeal rolls! It was very disappointing we really wanted them.

Given the poor food and service I believe we deserve a full refund. Please send a check for $82.58.

Sincerely,

Mrs. Becca Nowak

Check your answers on page 229.

POST-TEST

This test will give you a chance to see how much you remember about what you have studied. Take the test without looking in the book for help or answers.

The test has been divided into two sections. The first section is a test of your writing ability. It asks you to write a short essay. The second section is a test of your overall knowledge of the grammar, mechanics, and usage rules covered in this book.

Once you complete the test, check your answers on pages 207–210. Then fill out the Post-Test Evaluation Chart on page 206. The chart will tell you which sections of the book you might want to review.

Section I: Writing

Carefully read the assignments below. Pick *one* of these assignments to write about. Then use the writing process to write an essay about the topic of your choice. Begin by prewriting—planning what you want to say. Use your plan to write a first draft. Then revise and edit your draft.

ASSIGNMENT A: Narrative

On another piece of paper, write a narrative—a story about an event in your life. You can write about one of the following events or about another event of your choice.

▶ My first date
▶ My best (or worst) experience in school
▶ The craziest (or happiest) day of my life

Use time order to organize your narrative. End your narrative with a main idea sentence that sums up the point of your story.

ASSIGNMENT B: Example

On another piece of paper, write an essay in which you support a main idea with examples. You can write about one of the following topics or about another topic of your choice.

▶ Great (or terrible) bosses
▶ Co-workers' annoying habits
▶ Ways to entertain kids on a rainy day

Be sure that your essay begins with a clear main idea. Use order of importance to organize your examples.

ASSIGNMENT C: Persuasive

On another piece of paper, write a persuasive essay—an essay that tries to convince someone to do something or share your opinion. You can write about one of the following topics or about another topic of your choice.

► Why you are for (or against) having women serve in combat
► Why you are for (or against) stricter laws regarding smoking
► Why you are for (or against) mandatory jail sentences for drunk drivers

Be sure to state your opinion in a main idea sentence. Give good, convincing reasons to support your opinion. Organize the reasons effectively.

Section II: Grammar, Mechanics, and Usage

PART A: Nouns

This part tests your knowledge of common and proper nouns, singular and plural nouns, and possessive nouns. Underline and correct the error in each sentence.

► Several years ago, <u>America's</u> dream of space travel turned into a nightmare.

1. It happened in Florida in the Winter.

2. The Holiday season was scarcely over.

3. On tuesday, January 28, 1986, the space shuttle named *Challenger* exploded.

4. Peoples in many cities saw the tragedy on TV.

5. Americans wept to learn that seven astronaut had died.

6. To many Americans, the astronauts were true heros.

7. Men's and womens' faith in the space program was shaken.

8. A group of scientists was appointed by president Reagan.

9. The groups job was to look into the causes of the explosion.

10. The scientists report said that a seal had not worked properly.

11. This knowledge helped prevent other tragedys from occurring.

12. Everyone hoped that no more lifes would be lost.

PART B: Verbs
This part tests your knowledge of verb tenses, verb forms, and subject-verb agreement. Underline the correct form of the verb in parentheses.

▶ Can a mountain (<u>become</u>, becomes) a sculpture?

1. Mount Rushmore (stand, stands) in the Black Hills of South Dakota.

2. (Do, Does) you know about this monument?

3. Carvings of four presidential faces (exist, exists) in stone.

4. The giant sculpture (are, is) a famous landmark.

5. Its carving (start, started) in 1927.

6. The project (took, taked) fourteen years to finish.

7. The site (was chose, was chosen) by artist John Borglum.

8. He (wanted, has wanted) to use its fine granite.

9. Borglum made sure that he could (make, made) changes along the way.

10. He (has, had) a plaster cast to use as a model.

11. After workers (have, had) drilled holes in the rock, dynamite was inserted.

12. By the end of the project, workers (had blew, had blown) away more than 450,000 tons of rock.

13. Many people (went, gone) to watch the process.

14. President Roosevelt (saw, seen) the incomplete monument in 1936.

15. Work (was, were) still progressing when the artist died.

16. The (finish, finished) sculpture was unveiled by Borglum's son.

17. Over the years, the mountain (has became, has become) nationally known.

18. It will (continue, continued) to attract tourists.

PART C: Pronouns, Adjectives, and Adverbs

This part tests your knowledge of pronoun, adjective, and adverb forms and usage. Underline the correct form of the pronoun, adjective, or adverb in parentheses.

▶ Rockabilly music became (<u>popular</u>, popularly) in the 1950s.

1. Johnny Cash was one of its (best, bestest) performers.

2. Sun Records gave (he, him), Elvis Presley, and Jerry Lee Lewis their start.

3. Their music caught on (quick, quickly) with young people.

4. Cash and two friends formed (their, there) own band.

5. They called (themselfs, themselves) Johnny Cash and the Tennessee Two.

6. Success didn't come (easy, easily) for the group.

7. Singing for a living was (harder, hardest) than they expected.

8. At first, the band was paid hardly (nothing, anything).

9. Cash says (them, those) early days were rough.

10. With success, his days seemed (longer, more longer).

11. The (more hurried, hurrieder) his life got, the more pep pills he took.

12. The singer's life was more stressful than (mine, mine's).

13. Drug abuse caused problems between (he, him) and his wife.

14. It took a (terrible, terribly) accident to make Cash give up the pills.

15. Later, (he, him) and his wife won a Grammy.

PART D: Sentence Structure

This part tests your knowledge of different types of sentences and their punctuation. Each sentence has an underlined error. Circle the letter of the correct way to revise the error.

▶ What is a "wrap-around" <u>artist.</u>
   (a) artist?
   (b) artist!

1. Christo Javacheff is an <u>artist, who</u> creates his art by wrapping large objects.
   (a) artist. Who
   (b) artist who

2. In Paris, Christo covered the Pont-Neuf <u>bridge. With</u> huge sheets of yellow cloth.

  (a) bridge with

  (b) bridge. Using

3. What an amazing sight that must have <u>been.</u>

  (a) been!

  (b) been?

4. Christo also "wrapped" some small islands in <u>Florida they</u> looked like tropical flowers when viewed from the air.

  (a) Florida, they

  (b) Florida. They

5. Millions of people came to see the <u>bridge, thousands</u> of them left with a piece of the cloth.

  (a) bridge thousands

  (b) bridge, and thousands

6. The artist takes this <u>approach; because,</u> he wants to make people aware of what is around them.

  (a) approach because

  (b) approach. Because

7. Christo's huge works are <u>temporary. Which</u> has led to criticism from the art world.

  (a) temporary which

  (b) temporary, which

8. I can understand their <u>point however</u> I like Christo's work.

  (a) point; however,

  (b) point however,

PART E: Punctuation

This part tests your knowledge of basic punctuation rules. Add commas, colons, or semicolons where needed.

1019 Taylor Drive

Millard IL 60020

February 15 19_ _

Barry Cheung

Director of Human Resources

First National Bank of Triwood

2542 Financial Drive

Triwood IL 60000

Dear Mr. Cheung

I am writing in response to your ad of February 14 19–– in the *Triwood Times*. I believe that my background and experience and education qualify me for the position of manager trainee.

For the past five years I have held a variety of positions at United Financial a savings bank in Millard. As my resume shows I have successfully held the following positions teller teller supervisor customer service representative and consumer loan processor. My firsthand knowledge of these major areas of consumer banking would I'm sure be an asset in my role as a manager.

Moreover I would bring to the position a good understanding of both management and accounting. I will be receiving my B.S. in business management in June 19–– from Northern Business College. Before working on my B.S. I earned an associate's degree in accounting from Millard Community College.

Mr. Cheung I would appreciate an opportunity to discuss my qualifications in more detail. Please call me to arrange an interview my number is (708) 555-1122.

Sincerely yours,

Ed Rokowski

Ed Rokowski

Check your answers on page 209.

POST-TEST EVALUATION CHART

Use the Post-Test Answer Key on pages 207–210 to check your answers. Find the number of each question you missed in Section II of the Post-Test, and circle it in the Item Numbers column of the chart. Then look at the Review Pages column to see which pages you need to reread.

Grammar, Mechanics, and Usage	Item Numbers	Review Pages	Number Correct
Part A: Nouns			
Capitalization	1, 2, 3, 8	130–131	
Plurals	4, 5, 6, 11, 12	132–134	
Possessives	7, 9, 10	135–137	_____/12
Part B: Verbs			
Tense and Form	5, 6, 7, 8, 9	154–157	
	10, 11, 12, 13,	159–167	
	14, 16, 17, 18		
Agreement	1, 2, 3, 4, 15	150–153	_____/18
Part C: Pronouns, Adjectives, and Adverbs			
Adjective Form and Use	1, 7, 10, 11, 14	173–175	
Adverb Form and Use	3, 6	173	
Subject/Object Pronouns	2, 13, 15	140–142	
Possessive Pronouns	4, 12	144–145	
Reflexive Pronouns	5	146	
Demonstrative Pronouns	9	147	
Double Negatives	8	177	_____/15
Part D: Sentence Structure			
Sentence Types	3	179	
Compound Sentences	8	181–182	
Complex Sentences	1, 6	184–185	
Sentence Fragments	2, 7	186–187	
Run-Ons	4	183	
Comma Splices	5	183	_____/8
Part E: Punctuation			
Series	6, 11	189	
Dates and Addresses	1, 2, 3, 5	190	
Direct Addresses	15	192	
Appositives	8	191	
Interrupters	12	193	
Introductory Items	7, 9, 13, 14	194	
The Colon	4, 10	195	
The Semicolon	16	196	_____/16

POST-TEST ANSWER KEY

Section I: Writing pages 199–200

Evaluate your essay by answering the questions on the Evaluation Checklist below. If possible, also have a teacher, classmate, or friend evaluate your work. Then use the evaluations to revise your essay. If you need help revising, review the appropriate sections of this book.

Evaluation Checklist

Yes   No

☐ ☐ **1.** Does the essay have an introductory paragraph or paragraphs?

☐ ☐ **2.** Is the main idea clearly stated in the introduction? (Applicable to essays of example and persuasion. If the essay is a narrative, see Question 8.)

☐ ☐ **3.** Does the body contain at least one paragraph?

☐ ☐ **4.** Is the body developed with enough details to explain the main idea clearly?

☐ ☐ **5.** Do all the details in the body support the main idea?

☐ ☐ **6.** Are the details in the body logically organized?

☐ ☐ **7.** Is there a paragraph or paragraphs of conclusion?

☐ ☐ **8.** Does the conclusion help sum up the main idea? (If the essay is a narrative, does the conclusion include a main idea?)

☐ ☐ **9.** Are there any sentences or ideas that aren't clear?

☐ ☐ **10.** Are there errors in grammar, mechanics, or usage?

Section II: Grammar, Mechanics, and Usage

Part A: Nouns, page 200

1. **winter**—Do not capitalize the names of seasons.

2. **holiday**—*Holiday* is not capitalized because it is not the name of a specific holiday.

3. **Tuesday**—Capitalize the names of days of the week.

4. **People**—The plural of the irregular noun *person* is *people* (or *persons*).

5. **astronauts**—The clue word *seven* tells you that *astronauts* should be plural.

6. **heroes**—Singular nouns ending in a consonant and an *o* form the plural with an *es* ending.

7. **women's**—Irregular nouns form the plural possessive with an apostrophe and an *s* ('s).

8. **President**—*President* is capitalized because it is followed by a specific name.

9. **group's**—The job belongs to one group. Singular nouns form the possessive with an apostrophe and an *s* ('s).

10. **scientists'**—The report belongs to the scientists. Regular plural nouns form the possessive with an apostrophe after the final *s* (s').

11. **tragedies**—The plural of nouns that end in a consonant and a *y* is formed by changing the *y* to an *i* and adding *es*.

12. **lives**—For many nouns that end in *fe*, the plural is formed by changing the *f* to a *v* and adding *s*.

Part B: Verbs, page 201

1. **stands**—The subject, *Mount Rushmore,* is singular.

2. **Do**—*Do* agrees with the subject, *you.*

3. **exist**—The subject, *carvings,* is plural.

4. **is**—The subject, *sculpture,* is third person singular.

5. **started**—The action began and ended in the past.

6. **took**—The past tense of the irregular verb *take* is *took.*

7. **was chosen**—The passive voice requires the past participle form of this irregular verb.

8. **wanted**—The action began and ended in the past.

9. **make**—Main verbs do not change form when combined with a fixed-form helper such as *could.*

10. **had**—The action began and ended in the past.

11. **had**—The past perfect is needed to show that one action (drilling) occurred before another (inserting dynamite).

12. **had blown**—The past participle of the irregular verb *blow* is *blown.*

13. **went**—The past tense of the irregular verb *go* is *went.*

14. **saw**—The past tense of the irregular verb *see* is *saw.*

15. **was**—*Was* agrees with the subject, *work.*

16. **finished**—The verb is describing a noun and therefore must be in the past participle form.

17. **has become**—The past participle of the irregular verb *become* is *become.*

18. **continue**—Main verbs do not change form when combined with a fixed-form helper such as *will.*

Part C: Pronouns, Adjectives, and Adverbs, page 202

1. **best**—*Best* is the correct form of the adjective *good* to use when comparing more than two people or things.

2. **him**—The pronoun is an indirect object.

3. **quickly**—The adverb describes the verb phrase *caught on.*

4. **their**—The possessive pronoun is needed to show that the band belonged to Cash and his friends.

5. **themselves**—Plural reflexive pronouns end in *selves.*

6. **easily**—The adverb describes the verb *come.*

7. **harder**—Put an *er* ending on short adjectives used to compare two people or things.

8. **anything**—The sentence already contains a negative, *hardly.* Adding a second negative would create a double negative.

9. **those**—The sentence calls for a demonstrative, not an object, pronoun.

10. **longer**—When making a comparison, do not use both an *er* ending and the word *more.*

11. **more hurried**—Use the word *more,* rather than an *er* ending, with the two-syllable adjective *hurried.*

12. **mine**—*Mine* is the only possessive pronoun that doesn't end in *s.* None of the personal pronouns takes an apostrophe.

13. **him**—The pronoun is the object of the preposition *between.*

14. terrible—The adjective describes the noun *accident.*

15. he—The pronoun is part of a compound subject.

Part D: Sentence Structure, page 202

1. (b) The original sentence is punctuated incorrectly. Choice *b* is correct because the relative clause is essential. Choice *a* creates a sentence fragment.

2. (a) The original sentence contains a fragment. Choice *a* correctly joins the phrase to the sentence. Choice *b* creates another fragment.

3. (a) The original sentence has the wrong end mark. The exclamation point in Choice *a* helps show that the sentence should be read with emotion. Choice *b* incorrectly treats the exclamation as a question.

4. (b) The original sentence is a run-on. Choice *b* correctly separates the two independent clauses. Choice *a* creates a comma splice.

5. (b) The original sentence is a comma splice. Choice *b* correctly joins the independent clauses in a compound sentence. Choice *a* is a run-on sentence.

6. (a) The original sentence is incorrectly punctuated. Choice *a* correctly omits the punctuation from the dependent clause. Choice *b* creates a sentence fragment.

7. (b) The original sentence contains a fragment. Choice *b* correctly joins the relative clause to the independent clause. Choice *a* incorrectly omits the comma before the clause.

8. (a) The original sentence needs punctuation. Choice *a* is correctly punctuated. Choice *b* incorrectly omits the semicolon before the conjunctive adverb.

Part E: Punctuation, page 204

1019 Taylor Drive

(1) Millard, IL 60020

(2) February 15, 19– –

Barry Cheung

Director of Human Resources

First National Bank of Triwood

2542 Financial Drive

(3) Triwood, IL 60000

(4) Dear Mr. Cheung:

(5) I am writing in response to your ad of February 14, 19– –, in the *Triwood Times.* (6) I believe that my background and experience and education qualify me for the position of manager trainee.

(7) For the past five years, I have held a variety of positions at United Financial (8) , a savings bank in Millard. (9) As my resume shows, I have successfully held the following positions (10) : (11) teller, teller supervisor, customer service representative, and consumer loan

processor. (12) My firsthand knowledge of these major areas of consumer banking would, I'm sure, be an asset in my role as a manager.

(13) Moreover, I would bring to the position a good understanding of both management and accounting. I will be receiving my B.S. in business management in June 19–– from Northern Business College. (14) Before working on my B.S., I earned an associate's degree in accounting from Millard Community College.

(15) Mr. Cheung, I would appreciate an opportunity to discuss my qualifications in more detail. (16) Please call me to arrange an interview; my number is (708) 555-1122.

(*A period might also be used to separate the two independent clauses in the last sentence.*)

ANSWER KEY

Part I: Writing
Chapter 1: The Essay

Exercise 1, page 5
PART A
You can find job openings in a number of ways.

PART B
a

Exercise 2, page 7
PART A

(a) two bedrooms

(b) a big basement

(c) a fireplace in the living room

PART B
b

Exercise 3, page 9
PART A
My world seemed to turn upside down the day LaTise asked for a divorce.

PART B
b

Exercise 4, pages 12–13
PART A
Main idea: As a result of working with them, I've learned what it takes to be a good boss.

Main supporting detail, first paragraph of body: First of all, a good boss is fair.

Main supporting detail, second paragraph of body: A good boss also doesn't overload employees with work.

Main supporting detail, third paragraph of body: Finally, a good boss knows how to motivate people.

Restatement of main idea in conclusion: In short, a good boss is fair, reasonable, and a good motivator.

PART B
Supporting details and paragraphs will vary.

Chapter 2: The Writing Process

Exercise 5, page 23
PART A
Sentences will vary. Use these main idea sentences as guidelines for checking your own.

1. Here are some ways to cope when you're trying to quit smoking.

2. There are several good reasons to walk rather than drive.

3. Everything went wrong the day that I graduated.

PART B
Sentences will vary. If possible, have someone else read your main idea sentence to make sure that it's clear.

Exercise 6, page 25
PART A
1. **Group A: Good Points**
   (a) could come and go as I please
   (b) would feel good to be on my own
   (c) would have my own bathroom and bedroom
   (d) could play my music whenever I want
   Group B: Bad Points
   (a) will cost a lot
   (b) might be kind of lonely
   (c) hate to cook and clean

2.

PART B
Answers will vary.

Exercise 8, page 29
PART A
Answers may vary. Use these answers as guidelines for checking your own.
1. No—Though there's an opening paragraph, it doesn't really introduce the essay.
2. No—The introduction does not contain a main idea sentence. (The first sentence of the second paragraph would make a good main idea sentence.)

3. Yes

4. Yes—The details support the main idea, "I do the work of many people."

5. Yes

6. Yes

7. No

8. No

9. Yes

PART B
Answers will vary.

Take It Off!, page 29

Take It Off!

Are you tired of being <u>overweight</u>? Would you like to look and feel better? Here are some ways to lose those extra pounds.

Begin by building good eating habits. <u>Drink at least five glasses of water a day</u>. Water will help cut your appetite. Also, stay away from sugary and fatty foods. Instead, eat foods that are high in complex carbohydrates, such as potatoes and pasta.

<u>It's</u> also important to prepare yourself mentally. Each week, set a <u>realistic</u> weight-loss goal. For example, say you'll try to lose one pound. That way, you have something specific to aim for. When <u>you're</u> tempted to overeat, talk yourself out of it. Picture the thin person inside yourself just waiting to get out.

You also should try to exercise each day. Walk instead of driving. Climb the stairs instead of using the elevator.

Losing weight isn't easy. But you can do it if you really want to and know how. Follow the methods in this essay, and you, too, will lose weight.

Editing Exercise: Nouns, page 30

If you miss a correction, you may need to review the point of grammar behind it. In parentheses at the end of each sentence is the number of the page that explains the point. To review, read and complete the indicated page.

Dear Reba,

I received your letter in this <u>morning's</u> mail (page 135). It certainly brightened this chilly <u>Monday</u> (page 131). It's always great to hear from my favorite <u>aunt</u> (page 130).

We've had an unusually cold <u>fall</u> this year (page 131). An early <u>September</u> frost took us by surprise (page 131). Most <u>people's</u> gardens were ruined (page 137). You should have seen my poor <u>tomatoes</u> (page 133)! On the other hand, the <u>leaves</u> are especially colorful this year (page 133).

Bo and Nedra are really looking forward to <u>Halloween</u> (page 131). <u>Kids'</u> costumes were on sale at the dimestore, so I bought new ghost outfits (page 136). This year, we're going trick-or-treating with a few other <u>families</u> (page 133). It will be easier on me and more fun for the <u>children</u> (page 134).

Well, it's getting late and I have to pack tomorrow's <u>lunches</u>, so I'll sign off for now (page 133). Please give our love to <u>Uncle</u> Dan (page 130).

Chapter 3: Describing

Exercise 1, page 33

1. b

2. b

3. a

Exercise 3, page 37

1. from outside to inside

2. from far away to close up

3. from left to right

Check Your Understanding, page 40

PART A

1. b	**3.** a
2. a	**4.** b

PART B

1. Answers will vary. Use these answers as guidelines for checking your own.

Paragraph 4: "The boardwalk is like a ghost town."

Paragraph 7: "From this distance, it [the pier] looks as if it has been constructed of sticks by a child's hand."

2. Answers will vary. Use these answers as guidelines for checking your own.

Paragraph 6: "The roar and crash of the waves . . ." "The foam hisses like bacon frying."

3. Answers will vary. Use these answers as guidelines for checking your own.

Paragraph 4: "The sweet aroma of caramel corn that I remember from the summer has been replaced by the sharp, salty smell of the ocean."
Paragraph 16: ". . . I breathe the cool, clean-smelling air . . ."

4. Answers will vary. Use these answers as guidelines for checking your own.

Paragraph 7: "My sneakers sink into the sand."
Paragraph 8: "A head wind gently pushes against me."

Revision Warm-Up, page 45

Answers may vary. Use these answers as guidelines for checking your own.

1. No—Though there's an opening paragraph, it doesn't really introduce the essay.

2. No

3. Yes

4. No—because there isn't an overall impression.

5. No—There are a number of descriptive details, but the details don't add up to an overall impression. In addition, a few details are off the topic. Note, for example, the second sentence of paragraph 2.

6. Yes—In general, the details are in a logical order.

7. No—Though there's a closing paragraph, it doesn't really "wrap up" the essay.

8. No

9. No—Some sentences in paragraph 2 are confusing. Note, for example, the sentence "It rises from another."

Editing Exercise: Pronouns, page 46

If you miss a correction, you may need to review the point of grammar behind it. In parentheses at the end of each sentence with a correction is the number of the page that explains the point. To review, read and complete the indicated page.

Dear Linn,
It's too bad you couldn't make it to our New Year's Eve party (page 144). Glenn and I missed having you (page 143).

About twenty of our friends showed up. As usual, the Nielands brought their kids (page 144). I usually love children, but the Nieland kids

are so loud! They gave Glenn and me a headache (page 143). The Smiths sort of invited themselves (page 146). However, we didn't really mind. We enjoyed having them.

We decorated the living room with the silver streamers and balloons that you gave to us (page 142). Glenn and I put the long table on the right side of the living room (page 143). It was loaded with all kinds of food. Everyone loved Glenn's version of potato salad. Mine was less popular (page 145). However, those pizza puffs I made were gobbled up fast (page 147).

We're already beginning to plan next year's party, and we hope you can come. Put it on your calendar now!

Chapter 4: Narrating

Exercise 1, page 49
PART A

1. As I hugged my wife and kids, I was reminded of what really matters to me.

2. We would prove that people working together can get rid of gangs.

PART B
b

Exercise 2, page 51
PART A

1. a

2. c

3. b

PART B

1. person against self

2. person against nature

3. person against person

Exercise 3, page 53

1. 4, 3, 1, 2, 5

2. 5, 1, 4, 3, 2

3. 3, 4, 2, 1

4. 5, 1, 3, 2, 4

Check Your Understanding, page 56

PART A

1. a

2. c

3. 3, 1, 4, 5, 2

PART B

1. In the first two paragraphs, Malcolm X sets the stage by telling you the time, place, and situation.

2. Answers will vary. Use this answer as a guideline for checking your own.

As Malcolm X became aware that the whites in his town were racist, he began to dislike them.

Revision Warm-Up, page 61

Revisions of descriptive details and the main idea sentence may vary. Use these revisions as guidelines for checking your own.

Sky High

Last month, I found myself in a place I'd never been before. I was high over my hometown in a small plane piloted by my friend Carlos. ~~Carlos and I went to grade school together~~. I was terrified. My heart was pounding loudly in my ears, and I had closed my eyes so tightly that my forehead hurt. How did I get myself into this? I wondered.

Actually, I knew very well. My fear of flying was keeping me from a promotion. I was trying to overcome my fear.

"Are you OK?" Carlos asked. "I guess so," I said. But I was so scared that I was having trouble talking. Would I faint? I took a deep breath. Then, I pictured myself on the ground, victorious. The thought made me relax. Slowly, I opened one eye, then the other. I looked out the window and saw the most amazing sights. <u>I saw the whole community in miniature. My town seemed to be the size of a Monopoly game board. The houses and stores looked like pieces of the game.</u> To my surprise, I began to enjoy myself.

In no time at all, Carlos said, "We're landing." As I left the plane, my knees were wobbly but my head was clear. <u>It was one of my proudest moments. I had overcome my fear!</u>

Editing Exercise: Verbs, page 62

If you miss a correction, you may need to review the point of grammar behind it. In parentheses at the end of each sentence with a correction is the number of the page that explains the point. To review, read and complete the indicated page.

Back to School

I was really nervous about going back to school. My husband and kids <u>were</u> all for it (page 155). But I wasn't so sure. I <u>hated</u> school when I was a teenager (page 154). Would I hate it now? I also was afraid that I was too old for school. Then, I <u>ran</u> into an old friend (page 155). She said that she <u>was</u> taking high school classes through the library (page 157). She said that it was fun. She also said that age <u>doesn't</u> matter (page 152).

Now, my friend and I go to class two mornings a week. I am doing very well. I love school. My husband <u>says</u> he is proud of me (page 151). My kids <u>are</u> proud too (page 152). I never thought I could do so well.

Chapter 5: Explaining How

Exercise 1, page 65

Main idea sentence: Here are the steps a right-handed bowler should take.
Sentence that states a benefit: If you follow them, you'll improve your chance of bowling a strike.

Exercise 2, page 67

PART A

To <u>make</u> a California sandwich, <u>take</u> two pieces of wheat bread. <u>Spread</u> one piece of bread with a teaspoon of mayonnaise. Then, <u>put</u> a slice of Colby cheese on top of the mayonnaise. <u>Layer</u> lettuce, bean sprouts, and tomato on top of the cheese. <u>Cover</u> the sandwich with the second piece of bread and <u>cut</u> the sandwich in half.

PART B

Paragraphs will vary. Use this paragraph as a guideline for checking your own.

<u>Pick up</u> the receiver. Then, <u>listen</u> for the dial tone. Once you've <u>heard</u> it, <u>push</u> the buttons of the telephone number. <u>Wait</u> for someone to answer the phone.

PART C

Definitions will vary. Use these definitions as guidelines for checking your own.

▶ **Basting the hem**—to hold a hem in place temporarily by sewing it with a large running stitch

▶ **Bleeding the brakes**—to make sure that excess air has been removed from a car's break lining

▶ **Snapping the football**—to pass or hand the ball from the center to the quarterback, punter, or holder to begin a play

▶ **Choking the guitar string**—to pull the string upward to raise a note a half tone or pull it downward to lower the note a half tone

▶ **Creaming the butter and sugar**—to beat the mixture until it is light and fluffy

Exercise 3, page 69

1. 3, 1, 2, 6, 5, 4, 7

Paragraphs will vary. Use this paragraph as a guideline for checking your own.

To go grocery shopping, first make a list of what you need. Then, go to the store and get a shopping cart. Go up and down the aisles, selecting the food on your list. Next, empty your cart at the checkout and pay the cashier. Finally, take your food home.

Check Your Understanding, page 72

1. b

2. a

3. 6, 4, 1, 7, 3, 2, 5

4. a

5. b

6. Answers will vary but should include the following transitions: finally, then, until, when, now

Revision Warm-Up, page 77

Sit Up!

These days exercise is important. So is avoiding injury. Sit-ups can keep you fit, but you must be careful to do them properly.

It's important to start out in the correct position. <u>Lie on your back with your knees up and bent.</u> Keep your feet on the floor, about shoulder distance apart. Clasp your hands and rest them on the back of your neck.

Now, pull in your lower "tummy" muscles. At the same time, push your lower back into the floor. Your head and shoulders should naturally rise from the floor. <u>As you rise, breathe out.</u> Be sure to keep your head and elbows back and look toward the ceiling. Hold this position; then relax and lower your upper body. <u>As you lower, breathe in.</u>

Follow these steps, and you'll do sit-ups correctly. Soon, you'll have a firmer and more attractive tummy.

Editing Exercise: Verbs, page 78

If you miss a correction you may need to review the point of grammar behind it. In parentheses at the end of each sentence is the number of the page that explains the point. To review, read and complete the indicated page.

Two Different People

My ex-girlfriend and I <u>saw</u> eye to eye on very few things (page 163). One of the many things we couldn't <u>agree</u> on was movies (page 167).

She liked action pictures—the kind in which the bad guys are <u>killed</u> off by a hero (page 165). She wasn't happy unless a car or two and maybe a building were <u>blown</u> up during the course of the story (page 161). I have always <u>hated</u> violent pictures (page 159). I like upbeat, <u>well-written</u> stories about people overcoming their problems (page 166).

One Saturday night, our differences <u>came</u> to a head (page 162). We <u>had</u> just finished dinner and were arguing about what movie to see (page 160). She <u>had</u> been wanting to see an Arnold Schwarzenegger movie, whereas I wanted to see a movie about baseball (page 163). As we argued, each of us <u>grew</u> more stubborn (page 163).

Finally, we <u>did</u> the only thing we could do (page 162). We <u>went</u> to the same theater but not to the same movie (page 163). That very evening, we <u>broke</u> off our relationship (page 161). We haven't <u>spoken</u> to each other since (page 164). I should have <u>known</u> better than to date someone whose taste was so different from mine (page 163).

Chapter 6: Giving Examples

Exercise 1, page 81

Our kids see too much violence on TV.

Exercise 2, page 83

1. Mexican food is becoming more and more popular.
   ▶ Salsa now outsells ketchup.
   ▶ There are more than 50 Mexican restaurants in the city.
   ▶ Tortilla chips and salsa seem to be served at every party.

2. There's a national park for you, no matter what kind of landscape you like.
   ▶ There's the deep and vast Grand Canyon.
   ▶ There's the high, snowcapped Rocky Mountains.
   ▶ There's the huge, watery Everglades swamp.

3. Living in a country where you don't speak the language is difficult.
   ▶ Store clerks are impatient when they can't understand you.
   ▶ You can't understand what people are saying on TV shows.
   ▶ You can't ask for directions.

Exercise 3, page 85

b

Check Your Understanding, page 88

PART A

1. b

2. (b) Banking—third paragraph
   (c) Grocery shopping—fourth paragraph
   (d) Making long-distance phone calls—fifth paragraph
   (e) Taking elevators—sixth paragraph
   (f) Pumping gas—seventh paragraph

3. a

PART B

1. Answers will vary.

2. Osgood restates the main idea in paragraph 8: "It is clear now that when companies tell you they're doing things *better* now, they don't mean better for you. They mean better for them."

Revision Warm-Up, page 93

Revisions will vary. Use these revisions as guidelines for checking your own.

Bad Drivers

Every time I drive, I can't help noticing. Drivers are getting worse and worse. I'm surprised that the accident rate isn't higher than it is.

Too many people just don't pay attention to their driving. When they go to make a turn, they forget to use their turn signals. They're so busy changing the station on the radio or combing their hair that they don't seem to notice the light has changed. They also run stop signs.

Worse yet, many people also drive much too fast. I see tailgaters every time I drive on the highway. They're in such a hurry that they don't keep a safe distance from the other drivers. Speeding drivers have also made the side streets dangerous. The street I live on used to be quiet, but speeding cars have made it unsafe. The speeders just don't care about the kids playing near the street. Will it take a tragedy to make these drivers slow down?

I wish that our police department would do a more thorough job of finding and ticketing bad drivers. It's time we made our streets and highways safe again.

Editing Exercise: Adjectives and Adverbs, page 94

If you miss a correction, you may need to review the point of grammar behind it. In parentheses at the end of each sentence is the number of the page that explains the point. To review, read and complete the indicated page.

Picky Pet

My cat, Murphy, is the pickiest eater in the world (page 174). I've given her every brand of cat food on the market, and she doesn't like any of them (page 177). Each time that I give her a new brand, she acts as if it's the worst food she's ever eaten (page 175). Yesterday, I finally decided I had to do something to make her less fussy (page 174). I decided I wouldn't give her anything to eat until she'd cleaned her plate (page 177).

Last night, she began to meow pitifully (page 173). She hadn't touched the food I'd given her, and it looked terrible (page 173). It had been sitting so long that it was completely dry (page 173). She continued to meow sadly, but I pretended to ignore her (page 173).

Suddenly, I heard a loud noise in the kitchen (page 173). I quickly ran to see what had happened (page 173). Murphy had flipped her bowl over and was making the worst mess I'd ever seen (page 175). The cat meowed loudly and happily as I opened a can of tuna (page 173). I hated to give in, but I figured it was better than putting up with her tantrums (page 175).

Chapter 7: Comparing and Contrasting

Exercise 1, page 97

1. b
2. a

Exercise 2, page 99

Answers will vary. Use these answers as guidelines for checking your own.

COMPARISON AND CONTRAST CHART

Subject 1: Day Person		Subject 2: Night Person
HIGH	BASIS 1 ENERGY LEVEL IN MORNING	LOW
LOWER	BASIS 2 ENERGY LEVEL IN AFTERNOON	HIGHER
LOW	BASIS 3 ENERGY LEVEL AT NIGHT	HIGH

Exercise 3, page 101

1. b
2. a

Check Your Understanding, page 104

PART A

1. a
2. attitude toward TV, favorite drinks, dish-drying habits, favorite sports, food-buying habits, dinner times, blame for taxes, writing tools, Christmas cards
3. b

PART B

1. Rooney puts the main idea in the last sentence: "I thought it might help if I explained the difference between Republicans and Democrats."
2. Answers will vary.

Revision Warm-Up, page 109

Revisions will vary. Use these revisions as guidelines for checking your own.

Yesterday and Today

Recently, I had my twenty-sixth birthday. As I do on all my birthdays, I looked back on my past. The last ten years have been tough. However, I feel that my life is finally going in the right direction. I'm more mature now than when I was sixteen.

When I was sixteen, I was a know-it-all. My parents begged me to stay in school, but I ignored them. They seemed so hopelessly out of touch with the world and my life. Now that I'm twenty-six, I know my parents were right. As a dropout, I haven't been able to get very good jobs. To better myself, I've gone back to school. I know I have a lot to learn.

At sixteen, I had very little focus in life. In fact, I had only two goals. I wanted to get a job so I could buy a nice car and fancy clothes. And I wanted to be friends with the "right" people. In contrast, my goals today are very different. I don't care about fancy clothes or cars. I spend more time with family than with friends. Now, I want to get a good education and find a good job.

I still have a long way to go to reach my goals. But I know I will achieve them. I like myself better today than I ever have, and I believe my life is on the right track.

Editing Exercise: Sentence Structure, page 110

If you miss a correction, you may need to review the point of grammar behind it. In parentheses at the end of each sentence with a correction is the number of the page that explains the point. To review, read and complete the indicated page.

On My Own

Should I get my own apartment? (page 179) That was the question I kept asking myself. Finally, I decided to go ahead, and I rented my own place (page 181). Though it's expensive being on my own, it's well worth it (page 184).

I love the freedom of being independent. I answer to no one (page 183). I come and go as I please. If I come in at 3 o'clock in the morning, there's no one yelling at me, asking me where I've been (page 186).

I also enjoy my new-found privacy. When I lived at home, my little brother was always poking his nose in my business. I couldn't talk on the phone to my friends without my little brother listening in on our calls (page 187). Now, my life is much better (page 183). I'm able to keep private things private.

It's expensive to be on my own; however, I don't mind paying the price (page 182). I guess I'm just one of those people who are better off being on their own (page 186).

Chapter 8: Persuading

Exercise 1, page 113

1. When both husband and wife have full-time jobs, there's no reason why they can't share the household chores.

2. It's never too early for a child to learn to speak a second language.

3. By far, the best way to see the country is by motorcycle.

Exercise 3, page 117

1. **Opinion statement:** I think I know you well enough to say it: that guy's not right for you.
   Order: b

2. **Opinion statement:** If you elect me, I'll make this country better.
   Order: a

3. **Opinion statement:** Attend the auto show—there's no better way to spend a Saturday!
   Order: c

Check Your Understanding, page 120

1. **"Why I Am for the Death Penalty":** While there are many powerful arguments against the death penalty, I believe it is justifiable in many cases.
   "Why I Oppose the Death Penalty": The death penalty does not benefit society in any way.

2. a

3. Any two of the following answers are correct.
   Paragraph 2: No studies have proven that the death penalty curbs murder rates.
   Paragraph 3: Most murderers do not consider the consequences of their action.
   Paragraph 4: A life sentence is a more lasting punishment.
   Paragraph 5: Minority criminals are put to death in higher proportions than white criminals.
   Paragraph 6: The death penalty does not save taxpayers' money.
   Paragraph 7: The death penalty does not respect human life.
   Paragraph 8: The death penalty involves all of society in an unjustified act.

4. a

5. b

Revision Warm-Up, page 125

Revisions may vary. Use these revisions as guidelines for checking your own.

Lotteries Are a Waste

I think lotteries should be outlawed, or at least not allowed every day, for several reasons.

<u>First,</u> they're a waste of money, because your chances of winning are actually very small. I know people who like to play every now and then; I say, play for fun, but don't count on the money to pay your bills.

<u>Second,</u> they say the money goes for schools, but it seems like the schools still always need money. Maybe they should do a better job of managing the money they have. At any rate, lotteries clearly aren't the answer to school funding.

<u>Third,</u> people spend money they need for other things—groceries, kids, clothes—on lottery tickets. They're a temptation that many of us just don't need.

<u>In short, I don't think lotteries do people much good. They should be banned or at least be more limted than they are today</u>

Editing Exercise: Punctuation, page 126

If you miss a correction, you may need to review the point of grammar behind it. In parentheses after each correction is the number of the page that explains the point. To review, read and complete the indicated page.

September <u>1,</u> 19-- (page 190)

Miss Georgene Curtis
1920 South Grove
<u>Lincolnville,</u> KY 40272 (page 190)

Dear Miss <u>Curtis:</u> (page 195)
<u>For the past several months,</u> (page 194) you have been enjoying *Sportswrite,* America's leading sports magazine (page 191). But <u>now,</u> <u>Miss Curtis,</u> your subscription is about to expire (page 192). You have only until <u>October 1, 19--,</u> to take action (page 190). Don't let your subscription lapse! Just $12.99 buys you another twelve months of the best sports reporting.

Don't miss out on wonderful stories like <u>the following:</u> (page 195)
► "Is Baseball Doomed?"

▶ "You Pick 'Em: The Top Ten NFL QBs of All Time"

▶ "Foreman: Back in the Ring Again?"

<u>The most insightful stories</u>, <u>the most accurate predictions</u>, <u>the most complete statistics</u> are yours once again for the asking (page 189). <u>Just fill out the enclosed postcard; we'll bill you later</u> (page 196). (You can, <u>if you prefer,</u> (page 193) charge your subscription now.)

Chapter 9: Nouns

Identifying Nouns, page 129
PART A

1. man, woman, chefs, Chicago
2. Carlos, pastry, Star Café
3. Rita, sauces, restaurant, Oak Street
4. Carlos, Rita, jobs
5. Diners, food
6. man, cakes, parties
7. woman, spices, sauces
8. cooks, dream, future
9. Esquivels, place, years
10. restaurant, success

PART B
Answers will vary.

Capitalizing Nouns I, page 130

1. New Orleans, Louisiana
2. Luis, Tulane University
3. Lake Pontchartrain
4. Lee, Bourbon Street
5. French Quarter
6. Jackson Square
7. Uncle Jerome
8. Jerome, Congresswoman Jones
9. Hilton Hotel
10. Buddy Guy
11. Guy, Chicago
12. Preservation Hall
13. Paris Road
14. Jana, Mississippi River

Capitalizing Nouns II, page 131
PART A

1. Thanksgiving, Monday
2. Friday, Halloween
3. Saturday, Valentine's Day, Friday
4. New Year's Eve, May
5. January
6. Presidents' Day
7. Christmas
8. December

PART B
Answers will vary.

Identifying Plural Nouns, page 132
PART A

1. S
2. P
3. S
4. P
5. P

PART B
Hsu put out a stack of <u>napkins</u> for the whole family. Then Mr. Nurachi brought in several <u>bowls</u> of beans. The mother placed a pair of <u>chopsticks</u> by each plate. All <u>members</u> of the family sat down to eat.

Spelling Regular Plurals, page 133

1. lives
2. attorneys
3. families
4. shelves
5. Churches
6. tomatoes
7. beliefs
8. companies

Spelling Irregular Plurals, page 134

1. scissors
2. fish
3. mice
4. teeth
5. clothes
6. pants
7. people (*or* persons)
8. women

Forming Singular Possessives, page 135

PART A

1. author's
2. Tan's
3. mother's
4. Pallas's
5. daughter's
6. novel's

PART B

1. the novel's plot
2. the reader's interest
3. the book's cover

Forming Plural Possessives, page 136

PART A

1. tenants'
2. Golds'
3. families'
4. Schwartzes'
5. windows'
6. Smiths'
7. bedrooms'
8. landlords'

PART B

1. the attorneys' cases
2. several companies' products
3. the wives' complaints

Forming Irregular Possessives, page 137

PART A

1. the fishermen's boats
2. the children's toys
3. the women's uniforms
4. the two deer's tracks
5. those mice's tails
6. the people's choice

PART B

The <u>library's</u> collection of books and magazines is impressive. The friendly staff works hard to meet <u>people's</u> needs. The <u>children's</u> room has books, magazines, tapes, records, and computers. The room has won many <u>parents'</u> praise.

Chapter 9 Review, page 138

1. War
2. Bill
3. buddies
4. ambushes
5. Tuesday
6. Bill's
7. fall
8. women's
9. Men's
10. stereos
11. kids'
12. groups
13. lives
14. people
15. President
16. protests
17. University
18. Chicago
19. Park
20. Americans

Chapter 10: Pronouns

Identifying Pronouns, page 139

1. He, they
2. His
3. You
4. them
5. My, I
6. She
7. Her, himself
8. I, myself, them
9. We, our
10. It, our

Using Subject Pronouns, page 140

PART A

1. He
2. It
3. He
4. She
5. They
6. We
7. you
8. It

PART B

Sentences will vary. Use these sentences as guidelines for checking your own.

1. I would like to write a story.
2. She can help me think of a plot.
3. I hope that they like my story.
4. It will be about a mysterious castle.

Using Object Pronouns I, page 141

PART A

1. him
2. us
3. them
4. it
5. us
6. her
7. her
8. them
9. you
10. it

PART B

Sentences will vary. Use these sentences as guidelines for checking your own.

1. Please give him your attention.

2. We hired her to fill the managerial position.

3. They gave us a refund.

Using Object Pronouns II, page 142

PART A

1. her
2. him
3. it
4. them
5. us
6. you
7. it
8. it

PART B

He asked <u>me</u> to read my essay aloud. He also asked Yolanda to read her essay to <u>him</u>. Then he gave <u>her</u> constructive criticism.

Using Pronouns in Compounds, page 143

PART A

1. I
2. She
3. me
4. him
5. us
6. We, they
7. he
8. them

PART B

Neither their children nor <u>they</u> know how to cook it. So the children sometimes take <u>him</u> and her out to eat. You and <u>I</u> should go with them sometime.

Using Possessive Pronouns I, page 144

PART A

1. their
2. They're
3. It's
4. its
5. your
6. You're

PART B

Sentences will vary. Use these sentences as guidelines for checking your own.

1. Your job sounds very interesting.

2. His name is Hector.

3. The company changed its policy.

4. Their children are a joy to be with.

Using Possessive Pronouns II, page 145

PART A

1. Mine
2. yours
3. Hers
4. Theirs
5. ours

PART B

1. theirs
2. mine
3. his
4. yours

Using Reflexive Pronouns, page 146

1. myself
2. himself
3. themselves
4. me
5. itself
6. I
7. you
8. yourselves

Using Demonstrative Pronouns, page 147

PART A

1. that
2. Those
3. that
4. These
5. this

PART B

Sentences will vary. Use these sentences as guidelines for checking your own.

1. Please bring me that file.

2. These cookies are delicious.

3. We enjoyed those cookies that you brought last week.

Chapter 10 Review, page 148

1. its
2. He
3. himself
4. her
5. them
6. their
7. They
8. us
9. hers
10. those
11. me
12. This
13. I
14. mine
15. theirs
16. them
17. you
18. it's

Chapter 11: Verbs

Identifying Verbs, page 149

1. is
2. enlisted
3. worked
4. went
5. were formed
6. have served
7. has banned
8. know
9. do
10. pilot, assemble
11. are asking
12. face

Understanding Agreement, page 150

1. meet
2. serves
3. drive
4. live
5. quizzes
6. catches
7. confuse
8. start
9. helps
10. learn

Understanding Subject Nouns, page 151

1. He, plays
2. It, wins
3. He, makes
4. They, watch
5. She, sees
6. He, gives
7. It, supports
8. They, admire
9. He, sets
10. They, call
11. He, tries
12. We, love

Using *Be, Have,* and *Do,* page 152

1. is
2. are
3. has
4. is
5. has
6. does
7. am
8. do
9. are
10. have

Looking at Questions and Compounds, page 153

1. Are
2. are
3. have
4. is
5. Are
6. are
7. Do
8. likes
9. worry
10. is
11. take
12. Have

Forming the Past: Regular Verbs, page 154

1. decided
2. learned
3. dreamed
4. married
5. washed
6. started
7. renamed
8. mixed
9. straightened
10. changed

Forming the Past: Irregular Verbs, page 155

Many people <u>ran</u> the project. Folklorists from Indiana University <u>went</u> to Gary, Indiana. The folklorists <u>were</u> students interested in old customs. They <u>spoke</u> to people from different cultures. The folklorists <u>saw</u> how families followed traditions. The Meléndez family still <u>ate</u> Puerto Rican foods. Mrs. Meléndez <u>told</u> the group traditional folktales. Philip <u>wrote</u> down what she said. I <u>was</u> glad that I attended.

Forming the Future Tense, page 156

PART A

1. will stop
2. will join
3. will be
4. will meet
5. will do
6. will return

PART B

Sentences will vary. Use these sentences as guidelines for checking your own.

1. In a day from now, my candidate will win the election.
2. Next year, my son will learn how to drive.
3. Tomorrow, Rita will make dinner.

Forming the Continuous Tenses, page 157

PART A

1. were
2. was
3. are
4. am
5. Are
6. is

PART B
Answers will vary. Use these answers as guidelines for checking your own.

1. I am writing a letter.
2. I was sleeping.
3. I will be washing the dishes.

Chapter 11 Review, page 158

1. were
2. Are
3. were
4. look
5. was
6. ran
7. appeared
8. delighted
9. faded
10. are
11. will be
12. will become
13. rent
14. see
15. catches
16. tapes
17. shows
18. Do
19. has
20. watch

Chapter 12: More About Verbs

Using the Present Perfect, page 159

1. looked
2. has looked
3. have noticed
4. have complained
5. offered
6. refused

Using the Past Perfect, page 160

1. failed
2. stayed
3. turned
4. had filled
5. had burned
6. had wasted
7. phoned
8. had stopped
9. has worked

Using Irregular Verbs I, page 161

1. are, were, been
2. become, became, become
3. break, broken, broke
4. blows, blew, blown
5. brings, brought, brought

Using Irregular Verbs II, page 162

1. come, came, come
2. does, did, done
3. drinks, drank, drunk
4. eats, ate, eaten
5. freezes, frozen, froze

Using Irregular Verbs III, page 163

1. go, gone, went
2. grows, grown, grew
3. has, had, had
4. knows, knew, known
5. runs, run, ran
6. see, saw, seen

Using Irregular Verbs IV, page 164

1. speaks, spoken, spoke
2. steal, stole, stolen
3. take, took, taken
4. tells, told, told
5. writes, written, wrote

Forming the Passive Voice, page 165

1. kidnapped
2. imprisoned
3. stolen
4. rescued
5. praised
6. seen
7. complicated
8. faced
9. interrupted
10. taken

Using Participles, page 166

PART A

1. frozen
2. remodeled
3. revised
4. pleated
5. banned

PART B

Tom brought a huge bowl of <u>mashed</u> potatoes. Helene made her famous <u>pickled</u> beets. Gordon prepared a delicious casserole of <u>baked</u> sweet potatoes, apples, and sausage. I brought <u>buttered</u> carrots and peas. For dessert, Lena brought strawberry shortcake with <u>whipped</u> cream. Burton brought <u>poached</u> pears in a delicious sauce.

Using Fixed-Form Helpers, page 167

PART A

1. could use
2. must have
3. may attend
4. should take
5. can learn
6. might try
7. will start
8. shall go

PART B

Sentences will vary. Use these sentences as guidelines for checking your own.

1. Since I received my license, I can drive.
2. May I go with you?
3. We should exercise every day.

Chapter 12 Review, page 168

1. can look
2. have issued
3. might describe
4. known
5. was written
6. was limited
7. created

8. had defined
9. revised
10. have become
11. misspelled
12. had been
13. is done

Chapter 13: Adjectives and Adverbs

Identifying Adjectives, page 169

1. this
2. Few`
3. remote
4. main
5. seven
6. clay
7. huge
8. smaller
9. good
10. shorter
11. roof
12. storage
13. Korean
14. ancient
15. These

Finding Adjectives in Sentences, page 170

1. A, sensible
2. B, innocent
3. A, weird
4. B, strange
5. B, reasonable
6. B, one
7. A, illegal
8. A, funny
9. B, mountain
10. B, another
11. B, Debt
12. B, police
13. A, pointless
14. B, unusual

Identifying Adverbs, page 171

PART A

1. c
2. a
3. b

PART B

1. anywhere
2. negatively
3. immediately
4. well
5. very

Forming Adjectives and Adverbs, page 172

1. careful, carefully
2. soft, softly
3. strongly, strong
4. correct, correctly
5. pleasant, pleasantly
6. heavily, heavy
7. usual, usually
8. gentle, gently

Choosing Adjectives or Adverbs, page 173

PART A

1. loud
2. completely
3. hopeful
4. patiently
5. slowly
6. clearly
7. active
8. truly

PART B

Actually, his singing is <u>awful</u>. Everyone leaves the room <u>quickly</u> when Moshe starts to sing. If he sang quietly, it wouldn't be so <u>bad</u>. But his voice is <u>loud</u> enough to wake the dead!

Making Comparisons with Adjectives, page 174

1. tougher
2. least modest
3. most famous
4. strongest
5. faster
6. less skilled

Using Irregular Adjectives, page 175

PART A

1. worst
2. best
3. better
4. worst
5. worse

PART B

I think that the TV show was even <u>better</u> than the movie. The <u>worst</u> TV show was "My Mother the Car." It actually was <u>worse</u> than "Three's Company."

Making Comparisons with Adverbs, page 176

1. harder
2. less rapidly
3. more fully
4. better
5. most actively
6. more frequently
7. more quickly

Revising Double Negatives, page 177

1. a
2. a
3. b
4. b
5. b
6. a
7. b

Chapter 13 Review, page 178

1. whirling
2. most
3. worst
4. less
5. unbelievably
6. almost
7. Entire
8. any
9. immediately
10. best
11. tirelessly
12. impressive
13. more slowly
14. large
15. better
16. more
17. slowly
18. aren't

Chapter 14: Sentences and Punctuation

Using End Marks, page 179

1. !
2. .
3. . (or !)
4. ! (or .)
5. ?
6. .
7. .
8. ?

Understanding Simple Sentences, page 180

1. Most slave owners / didn't....
2. Mrs. Auld / broke....

3. This slave owner / taught....

4. Mr. Auld / beat....

5. Douglass / escaped....

6. He / began....

7. People / were inspired....

8. Douglass / wrote....

9. The book / is called....

10. You / should read....

11. Douglass / held....

12. He / served....

Understanding Compound Sentences I,
page 181

1. and

2. , so

3. , for

4. , but

5. or

6. , yet

Understanding Compound Sentences II,
page 182

1. ; moreover, (*Also correct are* furthermore *and* in addition.)

2. ; therefore, (*Also correct are* as a result *and* thus.)

3. ; however, (*Also correct is* on the other hand.)

4. ; furthermore, (*Also correct are* moreover *and* in addition.)

5. ; in addition, (*Also correct is* moreover *and* furthermore.)

6. ; otherwise,

Fixing Run-Ons and Comma Splices,
page 183

Corrections will vary. Use these corrections as guidelines for checking your own.

On the first day, the set worked fine; however, the picture disappeared the next day. Manoli thought the TV could be fixed. A repair shop was just down the street. The clerk said the set was old; therefore, they couldn't fix it. Manoli was disappointed. He didn't want to throw out the TV. The set wasn't really old, so why couldn't it be repaired?

The yellow pages had a list of repair shops. Others were advertised in the newspapers. Manoli called several, and his wife called the rest. A man at a shop said he could help, so Manoli took the TV in. The repair took only a few minutes. A tiny part had been broken. Manoli was pleased, and his TV worked for several years after that.

Understanding Complex Sentences I,
page 184

1. because no one is hiring

2. Until he finds employment,

3. while he was reading the paper

4. before he went to the store

5. After he made his list,

6. Though each coupon gave only cents off,

7. if he continues to use coupons

8. when you shop

Understanding Complex Sentences II,
page 185

1. that some adults believe in

2. , which are badly documented,

3. who believe in Bigfoot

4. , who worked for the Smithsonian Institution,

5. , which is similar to Bigfoot

Correcting Sentence Fragments I,
page 186

Corrections will vary. Use these corrections as guidelines for checking your own.

The problem lies in the growing cost of insurance premiums, which are too expensive for many people. Many children don't get proper medical care because parents can't afford it. Although many families still have medical insurance, they may not be able to pay for it in the future. Many people may suffer if something is not done soon. This problem has been recognized by many doctors, including C. Everett Koop, who used to be the surgeon general.

Correcting Sentence Fragments II, page 187

Corrections will vary. Use these corrections as guidelines for checking your own.

<u>A helpful and friendly salesclerk</u> showed Mrs. Ramirez several styles and colors. Mrs. Ramirez finally chose a green dress. <u>In a few minutes, she began trying it on.</u> It was too big! Her new diet had worked. <u>Mrs. Ramirez and the salesclerk both began laughing.</u> Then the two women looked <u>for a smaller-sized dress. Soon the pleased shopper selected and bought just the right dress.</u>

Chapter 14 Review, page 188

1. a	**6.** b
2. b	**7.** a
3. a	**8.** b
4. a	**9.** a
5. b	

Chapter 15: More About Punctuation

Punctuating Series, page 189

PART A

1. They plan to swim, run, play basketball, and work part-time this summer.

2. OK

3. June and Frank will work Mondays, Wednesdays, and Fridays at Hank's.

4. The three friends love the Mets, pizza, and going to concerts.

5. OK

PART B

Gas no longer seemed cheap or plentiful or something to take for granted after the oil crisis of the early 1970s. Some people began to commute in carpools, take public transportation, or bike to school or work. Others traded gas-guzzling cars for cheaper, smaller, more fuel-efficient models.

Punctuating Dates and Addresses, page 190

27 Lloyd Street
Minneapolis, MN 55401
July 25, 19--

Charlene Ramirez, President
Ramirez Tire & Auto, Inc.
430 W. Stoney St.
Boston, MA 02125

Dear Ms. Ramirez:

Your new year's offer of January, 19--, promised $50 back on any two Ramirez tires purchased during this year. Enclosed are copies of sales receipts for tires purchased in your Hibbing, Minnesota, outlet on October 17, 19--, and on July 10, 19--. Please send me the $50 rebate. Thank you.

Punctuating Appositives, page 191

1. She joined a theater group, the San Diego Repertory Theatre, and began to act in plays.

2. OK

3. In the film based on the novel, Goldberg played the role of Celie, an abused woman.

4. Steven Spielberg, the director of *E.T.: The Extra Terrestrial*, picked her for the role.

5. In *Ghost*, Goldberg played the role of Oda Mae Brown, the character who helps Demi Moore and Patrick Swayze reunite.

6. This role won her an important award, the Oscar for best supporting actress, and led to parts in other movies.

7. OK

Punctuating Direct Addresses, page 192

PART A

1. <u>Veronika and Ernesto,</u> please take out the garbage.

2. I voted for you, <u>Senator Hillman,</u> in the last election.

3. <u>Aunt Tereza,</u> I really appreciate the gift you sent me.

4. I care a great deal about you, <u>my friend.</u>

PART B

Sentences will vary. Use these sentences as guidelines for checking your own.

1. Run-D.M.C., where do you get your ideas for your songs?

2. I want you to know, Monica Seles, that I admire you.

3. I love your movie, Arnold Schwarzenegger.

Punctuating Interrupters, page 193

1. Many early factories were, by today's standards, terrible places.

2. Serious injuries were, in fact, common.

3. Certain practices, most notably locking exits to prevent stealing, led to disaster.

4. This method of theft control was dangerous, to say the least.

5. Workers were, unfortunately, trapped when fire broke out.

6. By the late 1800s, working conditions, though still bad, began to improve.

7. Workers, fed up with terrible conditions, had begun to join unions and organize strikes.

8. Unions have, of course, played an important role in the history of the U.S. worker.

Punctuating Introductory Items, page 194

1. In case of rain, the event will be held next Saturday.

2. However, the weather should be fine this week.

3. If you have the time, I hope you'll stop by.

4. Yes, we'll also be washing vans and motorcycles.

5. At the end of the day, we'll have a party at Sahana's house.

6. To make more money, our club will hold a bake sale later this year.

7. Once we make enough money, we'll be able to take a trip together.

8. OK

Using the Colon, page 195

1. Dear Editor:

2. OK

3. Gabriel's stats for the game were as follows: 26 points, 10 assists, and 3 rebounds.

4. Dear Marquez Cleaners:

5. The following students should report for class on Tuesday: Aaron, June, Cecily, and Raoul.

6. To Whom It May Concern:

Using the Semicolon, page 196

PART A

1. Football is a game of strength and speed; moreover, it takes brains and determination.

2. Marticka, Ever, and Guadalupe were there; however, Marilu, Gina, and Ron couldn't make it.

3. This tent had better be waterproof; otherwise, we'll be in trouble if it rains.

PART B

1. These shoes are too tight; my feet are killing me.

2. Jenna read the book *Another Country*; ask her about it.

3. Abandoned cars were everywhere; litter filled the street.

4. Gardening is her favorite pastime; she spends hours working in the dirt.

Avoiding Common Punctuation Errors, page 197

1. Mr. Wong, whom we met last weekend, is from Taiwan.

2. Ben Harrison, the man downstairs, is from England.

3. The family that owns this liquor store, is from India.

4. OK

5. Our neighborhood holds, a street fair each summer.

7628 North Willard Street
Chicago, IL 60648

April 8, 19--

Yoder's Restaurant
5323 Wyman Way
Elmhurst, IL 60126

Dear Mr. Yoder:

I have enjoyed eating in your restaurant for many years. However, I had a terrible experience there last night. My husband, two friends, and I had reservations for 8:00 P.M. and arrived right on time. Much to our annoyance, the hostess, Loretta Smith, told us our table was not ready. Mr. Yoder, we then waited 45 minutes. We wanted our friends to try your cornmeal rolls; otherwise, we would have left.

Finally, we were seated. But our troubles were not over. During the course of the meal, we suffered through the following problems: warm salad, cold soup, and a waiter who dropped a drink in my husband's lap. Furthermore, we learned that you no longer serve cornmeal rolls! It was very disappointing; we really wanted them.

Given the poor food and service, I believe we deserve a full refund. Please send a check for $82.58.